Recipes from Historic
COLORADO

Other Books by the Authors

Recipes from Historic America

Recipes from Historic Louisiana

Recipes from Historic Texas

The Great American Sampler Cookbook

At Ease in the White House

The New American Sampler Cookbook

The American Sampler Cookbook

How to Sell to the United States Government

The Homeschool Handbook

Recipes from Historic
COLORADO

A Restaurant Guide and Cookbook

LINDA & STEVE BAUER

Taylor Trade Publishing
Lanham • New York • Boulder • Toronto • Plymouth, UK

If you would like to share comments about the book, ask the authors to lecture for your group, or you desire autographed copies, please contact us at bauerbooks@gmail.com

Published by Taylor Trade Publishing
An imprint of The Rowman & Littlefield Publishing Group, Inc.
4501 Forbes Boulevard, Suite 200, Lanham, Maryland 20706
www.rlpgtrade.com

Distributed by National Book Network

Library of Congress Cataloging-in-Publication Data
Bauer, Linda.
 Recipes from historic Colorado : a restaurant guide and cookbook / Linda Bauer and Steve Bauer.
     p. cm.
 Includes index.
 ISBN-13: 978-1-58979-378-1 (cloth : alk. paper)
 ISBN-10: 1-58979-378-1 (cloth : alk. paper)
 1. Cookery. 2. Cookery—Colorado. 3. Restaurants—Colorado—Guidebooks. 4. Historic buildings—Colorado—Guidebooks. I. Bauer, Steve, 1943– II. Title.

TX714.B3787 2008
641.59788—dc22   2007049501

∞™ The paper used in this publication meets the minimum requirements of American National Standard for Information Sciences—Permanence of Paper for Printed Library Materials, ANSI/NISO Z39.48–1992.
Manufactured in the United States of America.

Dedication

With much love we dedicate this book to Linda's Mom—though she left this life many years ago, she is never forgotten. To our sons Mike and Chris, who gave us such great memories of skiing, snowboarding, fishing, hiking, and horseback riding in this fantastic year-round paradise called Colorado. To our beloved relatives, who reside in this state and are part of the reason it is such a fine place to live and love!

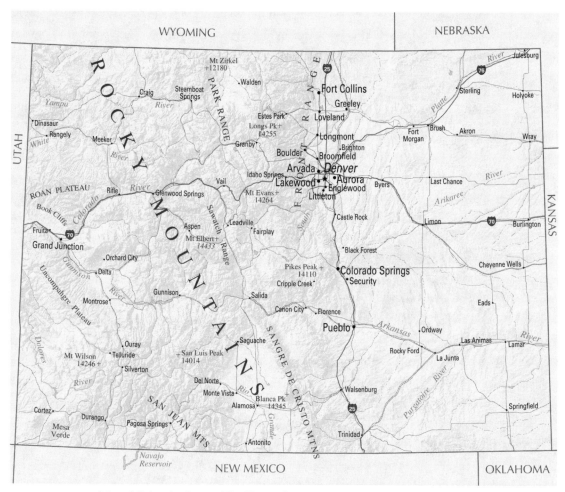

Map of Colorado. Source: The National Atlas of the United States of America.

CONTENTS

ACKNOWLEDGMENTS

To make all of our dreams come to fruition, some of the very finest people have been laboring with us for years on this mammoth project. *Recipes from Historic Colorado* could not have come to pass without the support of our publisher and friend, Rick Rinehart of Taylor Trade Publishing. How great it is to partner with him once again.

Our deepest gratitude to the many individuals throughout Colorado who serve up some of the finest food, relaxing accommodations, and spectacular history in each of the over 40 establishments that we chose to highlight in this book. May your days be pleasant and your rooms and tables full of happy, loving guests.

Special thanks to Natalie Martinez, Rich Grant, Meredith Arndt, Holly Johnson, the Pringles, Susan Jessup, Cheri and Jerry Helmicki, and the Van Berkum family. We will never forget your special kindness, attention to detail, and true spirit of the West. To Bob Scott—you are the best and brightest. I hope that Grand Lake Lodge appreciates the unprecedented devotion that you bring. I will never forget meeting you and learning so much.

To our editors, Elaine McGarraugh and Chris Thillen; to the art directors and designers; and to all the crew who gave their utmost time and talents. Thank you—until we meet again!

INTRODUCTION

Few people are able to truly follow their passion. Therefore the opportunity to thoroughly visit and delight in the people of a particular state—as well as share their history, mystery, and culinary achievements—has been a real blessing for our family. We have truly enjoyed striving to share the state with each of our readers.

Through this series of books we have had the pleasure of exploring Texas, Louisiana, California, and our favorites of America. For twenty-two years our family has been able to travel throughout the world, sharing the joy of exploration as well as learning about cultures and sports, making new friends, and experiencing the joys of each area's food and festivals.

Recipes from Historic Colorado was a simple choice. This beautiful state beckoned us from the beginning. Each season offers different sports, flora, fauna, and fantastic food. From our first time on a Grand Circle tour for two weeks throughout the West, Christopher, our son, and I realized what a gem was included in areas such as Telluride. He skied on snowcapped mountains. Later we loved the historic Chop House with its wild game dishes and historic hotel. Celebrities flock to the area for good reason—the resemblance to Switzerland is uncanny.

A Colorado cowboy once said, "You can rub out cow trails with highways, swap sagebrush for cities and free-range grass for filling stations, but you can't cure the west of bein' 'howdy country.'" Another piece of cowboy wisdom says that "the cowboy inhabits a world of his own language, customs, humor, principles, ways of doing things, manner of thinking." This is true of dude ranches, and each one offers its own particular Western experience and distinct Western atmosphere.

On such an excursion, all four of us experienced an amazing time visiting several historic dude ranches. We just wish every family could enjoy the incredible odyssey of family fun by horseback riding together, then fishing and possibly catching dinner at Rainbow Trout Ranch. The chef actually cooked our catch for all to share in an excellent meal together. Fond memories of rocking on the lodge deck while counting the hundreds of hummingbirds and playing a game of horseshoes are truly priceless. Later, staying up to watch shooting stars from the porch of your cabin is the absolute ultimate!

Upscale properties also abound, and a visit to Devil's Thumb Ranch will have you returning as I did. Bob and Suzanne Fanch have created a true paradise, while carefully preserving the environment. Bob has made a fortune in the cable industry, yet when we met he was busy helping the construction workers. Once again the spirit of Colorado emanates from his soul, as he treasures the land and the people.

Another trip included our sons, Michael and Chris, taking the Ski Train from Denver to the slopes of Winter Park where expert skiers taught them to enjoy snowboarding. We also discovered that Winter Park has a world-class program for handicapped skiers.

I must share the generosity of my cousin, Marcia Murphy Lortscher, the longest-living diabetic kidney recipient in the world. This Denver native happens to be blind and has beaten cancer twice. Others might find this a tough road to hoe; yet she has the most positive, Colorado, can-do spirit. She has donated the money for the incredible Dialysis Center of YMCA of the Rockies near Winter Park. I have yet to see a finer place for family fun, and now it is a way for those who need dialysis to join their families and feel comfortable and cared for while enjoying the Colorado sports.

Lastly, our wonderful publisher Rick Rinehart makes his home in this incredible state. He fully understands and knows the true beauty that inspired the writing of "America the Beautiful!"

Denver

THE BROWN PALACE HOTEL

The red granite and sandstone walls of The Brown Palace have watched more than a century of Colorado and Denver history develop. The city was a mere 34 years old when Henry C. Brown opened the doors of his monument to himself in August 1892. It was a braggart city built by men who had made fortunes based on the gold and silver drawn from the mountains they then viewed from mansions on Capitol Hill where Brown had first homesteaded. They welcomed the new, elegant locale in which to conduct their business deals. Their wives took tea and their daughters danced at lavish balls.

It was fittingly a palace for "The Queen City of the Plains," as Denver dubbed itself. Inside the hotel designed by architect Frank E. Edbrooke, the eight-story atrium, its pillars and wainscoting of pale golden onyx from Mexico reflecting the pastel shades of the stained glass ceiling, rivaled the grandest of hotels "back East." A massive fireplace, the mantel of which was supported by two solid pillars of onyx, was a welcome amenity when the winter winds howled down from the snowcapped peaks to the west.

Through the years, The Brown Palace has seen it all—boom times and depressions, peace and war. If the walls could talk, what stories they would tell of love and betrayal, success and failure, happiness and despair.

Emperors, kings, and presidents have been closeted here. Royal queens and the goddesses of stage and screen have primped in these rooms. We can only imagine some of their stories. Others we know.

Teddy Roosevelt was the first president to stop at The Brown Palace Hotel. He came to Colorado to hunt bear in the spring of 1905. He spoke to businessmen who paid only $10 to attend. Perhaps this was the prelude to "smoke-filled rooms." Fifteen hundred cigars were smoked during the event.

President and Mrs. Eisenhower were the most frequent First Family to visit The Brown Palace. It served as his pre-campaign headquarters in 1952, and they spent many of their summer vacations here. In 1955, President Dwight D. Eisenhower had a travel allowance of $40,000 per year. A reporter estimated that an eight-week vacation in Denver would cost $25,000, including lodging and meals for his staff and Secret Service agents. To commemorate their many visits, the former Presidential Suite was renamed the Eisenhower Suite in 1980. A wayward golf ball Ike hit while practicing in the room made the dent in the fireplace mantel. The dent remains today. Eisenhower stories are recounted during the twice-weekly historical tours.

A report during President Harding's stay in July 1923 said that "the White House for a few hours is on the eighth floor of The Brown Palace Hotel, and it will hold this temporary site until the party resumes its western jaunt at 1:30 o'clock this afternoon."

In the 1890s, a German count who had been banned from home over a small indiscretion ran out of funds while living it up in the United States. He worked as a bookkeeper at The Brown Palace for over a year. In 1903 Count D'Agreneff, a Russian nobleman, worked as a barber at the hotel and shaved President McKinley when he visited Denver. Another royal employee was Baron Gottfried von Kroenberger, a WWI ace for Germany who flew with Von Richtofen. He was head waiter when the hotel opened the Palace Arms in 1950.

Sun Yat Sen, just prior to being appointed the first president of the New Republic of China in 1911, was in Denver raising money to free his countrymen from the Manchu Dynasty. While he was staying at The Brown Palace, the revolution broke out and a republic was proclaimed. Years later Dr. Sun Yat Sen was recognized in a special five-cent postage stamp issued July 7, 1942, to commemorate China's five-year resistance to WWII Japanese aggression.

When Queen Marie of Romania visited Denver in 1926, she attended many royal functions, including a banquet at The Brown Palace Hotel. It was said that one of the reasons for her visit was to raise money to bolster her country's sickly finances. It is not surprising then that she spent an hour at the Denver Dry Goods store downtown to endorse a new line of vacuum cleaners.

More than 700 wrought iron grillwork panels ring the lobby from the third through the seventh floor. Two of them are upside down, one to serve the tradition that man, who cannot be perfect, must put a flaw into his handiwork; the other sneaked in by a disgruntled workman. Finding these bits of history intrigues visitors to the 112-year-old Brown Palace.

The Brown Palace Hotel
321 17th Street
Denver, Colorado 80202
(303) 297-3111

4 pounds beef tenderloin

1 teaspoon salt

pepper to taste

1 cup duxelles (recipe follows)

Optional: 2 tablespoons diced
truffles

1 puff pastry sheet

2 pieces of sandwich bread,
toasted

½ cup egg wash (2 whole eggs,
whisked)

2 envelopes of sauce Madeira,
prepared according to
directions

DUXELLES

2 cups finely chopped
mushrooms

2 cups finely chopped shallots

salt and pepper to taste

white wine, enough to moisten

Beef Wellington

Season and sear tenderloin. Cool. Combine duxelles and truffles. Spread evenly on one side of the tenderloin. Roll out dough to 3/16 inch thick. Lay tenderloin with duxelles spread face down on dough in the center. Spread duxelles on top side of tenderloin. Trim toasted bread and size it to lie on top of the tenderloin. Fold pastry on top and brush with the egg wash. Rotate wrapped tenderloin so bottom side is now facing up and meat is now sitting on top of the toasted bread pieces.

Trim sides of pastry and then fold under. Use egg wash to seal seams. Decorate with pastry scraps as desired. Bake at 350 degrees for 40–45 minutes. Dough should be cooked through and golden brown. Meat should have an internal temperature of 115 degrees for medium rare. Cut into ¾-inch slices. Serve the prepared sauce Madeira on the side.

DUXELLES

Mix together and sauté in 1 tablespoon butter. It should be moist enough to hold together, but not runny.

YIELD
Serves 10

Crepes Suzette

CREPES

Mix together all ingredients except butter. Strain through a fine mesh sieve and let rest overnight.

Add melted butter to mixture and thin with milk if necessary to a consistency where it coats the back of a spoon. Coat a nonstick sauté pan evenly with batter and cook over medium heat until lightly brown. Turn over and briefly finish. Set aside. Continue to make crepes one at a time.

SUZETTE

In a pan, over medium heat, melt butter. Add sugar and cook for 30 seconds. Squeeze orange and lemon halves to completely juice them. Add Cointreau. Cook mixture to a syrupy consistency for approximately 1 minute. Add crepes and turn over once. Carefully add Grand Marnier and then flambé.

Remove crepes to plate. Scoop chocolate and/or vanilla ice cream on top of crepes. Spoon leftover syrup on top. Garnish with mint chiffonade, kumquat halves, and orange zest, if you like.

YIELD
Serves 4

CREPES

6 eggs

1 quart whole milk

½ cup sugar

4 cups flour

zest of 2 oranges, finely minced

¼ stick butter, melted

SUZETTE

1 tablespoon butter

1 orange, split in half and wrapped in cheesecloth

½ lemon, wrapped in cheesecloth

2 tablespoons sugar

2 tablespoons Grand Marnier

1 tablespoon Cointreau

New England Seafood Chowder

8 ounces bacon, diced small

1 whole onion, diced small

2 celery stalks, diced small

2 cups potatoes, peeled and diced

2 teaspoons chopped fresh garlic

1 large can chopped clams

1 large can clam juice

2 cups chicken broth

1 teaspoon dried thyme

1 bay leaf

1 pinch cayenne pepper

1 pinch white pepper

4 ounces butter

1 cup all-purpose flour

salt and pepper to taste

2 cups heavy cream

8 ounces fresh seafood, including large diced salmon, shrimp, fresh cod

olive oil

In a large pot, render diced bacon until crisp. Add onions, celery, and garlic. Add 4 ounces of butter and glaze onions, celery, and garlic. Add 1 cup of flour and soak up all the fat. Add cold clam juice slowly and whisk so no lumps are able to form. Add chicken broth and cream. Season with salt, white pepper, and cayenne pepper. Add bay leaf and dried thyme and simmer for about 20 minutes so the raw flour taste disappears. Add chopped clams and diced potatoes and cook for another 15 minutes until potatoes are soft.

Season the fresh seafood and sauté quickly in olive oil. Drain oil and add the seafood to the chowder.

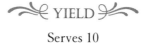

YIELD
Serves 10

"Part of the secret of success in life is to eat what you like, and let the food fight it out inside."

—Mark Twain

BUCKHORN EXCHANGE

Colonel William F. "Buffalo Bill" Cody met Henry H. Zietz in 1875 when Henry was only 10 years old. Two years later, at the age of 12, Henry was a working member of Buffalo Bill's band of scouts. Cody had been a soldier in the Union Army in Kansas and had worked his way up to non-commissioned officer before the war ended. He later was drawn back to the military when he was offered the position of Chief of Scouts for the Fifth Cavalry by General Sheridan.

Having quickly accepted the honor, Cody promptly encountered a herd of buffalo while leading the regiment. After killing several, he was immediately recognized by the commanding officer as an able hunter. When he was sent out the following day for more buffalo, he requested wagons to bring the carcasses back to camp. The colonel refused, saying he had to kill them first, which he ultimately did rather quickly. Two days later, when sent on the same supply mission, Cody did not bother to ask for wagons. Instead, he found a herd of buffalo and drove them alive into the Cavalry camp and shot them there, telling the colonel he wanted the buffalo to provide their own transportation. He was dubbed Buffalo Bill, and the name stuck.

As a scout, Henry Zietz was a success despite his diminutive stature. Having made the acquaintance of Chief Sitting Bull, who became rather fond of Henry due to his friendliness and honesty in dealing with the Indians, he was affectionately referred to as "Shorty Scout." Sitting Bull, Buffalo Bill, and Shorty were friends for life. Years later, Sitting Bull's nephew and 30 Sioux and Blackfoot Indians ceremoniously rewarded Shorty with the military saber taken from General George Custer at the Little Big Horn. The sword remains in the Zietz family today.

Scouting life required constant travel, so Shorty settled down by opening the Buckhorn Exchange in 1893. Now Denver's oldest and most historic eating and drinking emporium, it has been in operation for over a century. The Buckhorn Exchange has liquor license Number One, issued by the State of Colorado at a cost of $25. From the first day the establishment opened, silver barons, gamblers, cattlemen, railroad men, miners, entrepreneurs, roustabouts, and a few Indian chiefs stopped by for a drink and a meal at the Buckhorn.

Teddy Roosevelt came for a meal and then went hunting with Shorty as his guide. They became such good friends that Shorty accompanied the president on his next hunting trip to Africa. Other notable visitors have been Presidents Reagan, Eisenhower, and Carter, Charlton Heston, Roy Rogers, James Cagney, Bob Hope, Will Rogers, and Princess Anne of Great Britain. John F.

8

Kennedy's fishing license is framed on the wall. More than 500 trophy animal heads are mounted around the restaurant and bar, and the collection of antique guns is exceptional.

Prohibition was implemented in Colorado in 1916, three years before the rest of the nation. To survive, the front of the saloon was turned into a grocery. Presumably, this ran as a profitable business venture, but legend says that Shorty would sometimes hollow out a loaf of pumpernickel bread and fill the cavity with a bottle of bootleg whisky for his special customers. Other stories tell of a hidden passage to the second floor, where select patrons might avoid the inconvenience of a police raid.

When Henry H. "Shorty Scout" Zietz died in 1949, he was recognized as one of the most colorful figures of the early West. The last of Cody's famous scout band was gone. His son, Henry Jr., operated the Buckhorn until the present management purchased it from the Zietz family in 1978.

The new management has taken great care to preserve the memorabilia of Colorado's history, and they were careful not to disturb the basic exterior of the structure. The Buckhorn Exchange was designated a historic landmark by the City and County of Denver in 1972. The magnificently ornate white-oak bar and back bar, made in Essen, Germany, in 1857 and brought to Denver by Shorty, were relocated to the second floor where they are the centerpieces of the Buckhorn's Victorian lounge. Any trip to Denver must include a stop at the Buckhorn.

Buckhorn Exchange
1000 Osage Street
Denver, Colorado 80204-3918
(303) 534-9505

Prime Rib of Buffalo
with Seven-Seed Crust

One day prior to cooking, remove the roast from refrigerator. Trim all exterior fat to ⅛ inch, and tie it between the rib bones in order for roast to hold its flavor.

Rub exterior of the rib with a small amount of olive oil until evenly coated. Place the seeds, peppercorns, and salt in a blender or spice grinder and process until the consistency of coarse cornmeal. Evenly coat the roast with the spice blend and return to refrigerator for about 24 hours.

When ready to cook, preheat oven to 425 degrees. Place the roast in a shallow pan and place in the oven for 20 to 30 minutes until the seeds are roasted to a deep brown. Reduce the oven temperature to 325 and continue to cook until the meat reaches an internal temperature of 120 degrees.

Remove from the oven and let stand for 15 minutes. Remove the roast from pan; place it on a cutting board and cover with foil and a kitchen towel. Pour the pan drippings through a mesh strainer filled with lots of ice into a small saucepan (this will remove the excess

1 buffalo prime rib (6–7 pounds)

olive oil

1 tablespoon anise seeds

1 tablespoon whole coriander seeds

1 tablespoon fennel seeds

1 tablespoon mustard seeds

1 tablespoon celery seeds

1 tablespoon Tellicherry peppercorns

1 tablespoon green peppercorns

1 teaspoon sea salt

1 cup beef stock

1 cup fine Cabernet

grease). Place the saucepan on the stove and add the beef stock. Add the Cabernet and bring to a boil, then reduce to a simmer.

Remove the rack of bones and slice into servings of desired thickness or number. Serve au jus.

❦ YIELD ❧

Serves 10–12

Buffalo Redeye Stew

Place potato cubes in saucepan, cover with water, and bring to a boil. Reduce heat to simmer and continue to cook until potatoes are about half done. While potatoes are simmering, melt butter in a large saucepan over medium heat; then add stew meat, onion, and dry spices. Allow to simmer while potatoes are cooking. When potatoes are about half done, add flour to pan with buffalo and mix well. Allow to cook for 5 minutes.

Add the can of tomatoes to the buffalo mixture and stir. Let simmer for 5 minutes. Drain potatoes; add the balance of ingredients, gently stirring together. Return to a boil, reduce heat, and allow to simmer for 30 minutes or until buffalo is tender. Serve in a large, hollowed-out loaf of sheepherder's bread or your favorite bread.

4 potatoes, peeled and cut in 1-inch cubes

¼ pound butter

2 pounds buffalo stew meat, preferably sirloin

½ yellow onion

¼ tablespoon white pepper

¼ tablespoon leaf thyme

¼ tablespoon whole rosemary

¼ tablespoon basil

1 cup flour

28 ounces diced tomatoes

½ tablespoon salt

1½ tablespoons granulated garlic

½ cup bourbon

½ cup strong coffee

1 tablespoon Worcestershire sauce

2 cups water

12

½ pound butter

½ pound powdered sugar

¼ teaspoon real vanilla

1 teaspoon cinnamon

1 teaspoon dark rum

Buckhorn Exchange Cinnamon Rum Sauce

When winter weather whirls outside, stay warm with a sweet touch of Dutch apple pie topped with the Buckhorn Exchange's cinnamon rum sauce.

Combine all ingredients in a bowl and mix on low speed until well blended. Increase mixer speed and continue mixing until volume doubles. Serve over your favorite hot Dutch apple pie. Top pie and sauce with vanilla ice cream if desired—or better yet, drop by the Buckhorn for this signature dessert.

"I look upon it that he who does not mind his belly, will hardly mind anything else."

—Samuel Johnson

Cumin-Crusted Lamb Lollipops
with Baby Garbanzo Salad

Combine all spices in a large Ziploc bag. Rub the rack of lamb with spices and refrigerate in the bag overnight.

Just before serving the next day, preheat oven to 350 degrees and cook the lamb until it reaches an internal temperature of 135 degrees. Remove lamb from the oven and let rest for 15 minutes. Cut into single chops, arrange on a platter around the salad, and serve.

SALAD

In a heavy-bottomed saucepan, bring water to a boil with the garbanzo beans, then simmer for about 30 to 40 minutes until the beans are tender. Remove from heat and drain the beans. Rinse the beans to keep them from sticking. In the same saucepan, heat 1 tablespoon of olive oil and lightly sauté the garlic and red pepper. Remove from heat, toss the mixture with the garbanzo beans, and let cool. Add herbs, 1 tablespoon olive oil, and the lime juice. Season with salt and pepper to taste. This dish should be served at room temperature.

 YIELD

Makes 2 dinners or 7 appetizers

1 lamb rack (approximately 7 bones)

1 teaspoon ground cumin

½ teaspoon salt

¼ teaspoon ground coriander

1 pinch white pepper

SALAD

1 cup dry baby garbanzo beans

3 cups lightly salted water (or use vegetable or chicken stock)

¼ cup fresh chives

1 teaspoon fresh rosemary, minced

2 tablespoons fresh mint, minced

¼ cup diced red pepper

1 tablespoon. fresh lime juice

2 tablespoons olive oil

½ teaspoon fresh minced garlic

salt and pepper

Buffalo Crostini

7 ounces sun-dried tomatoes

4 tablespoons capers

8 green onions, finely chopped

2 tablespoons balsamic vinegar

thinly sliced buffalo rib eye, prime rib, or other meat

thinly sliced baguette or toasted bread rounds

This is a perfect appetizer for parties—other meats can be substituted for buffalo.

Mix together the first three ingredients with balsamic vinegar. Set aside and toast the bread rounds under a broiler until golden brown. Place thinly sliced buffalo or other meat atop bread rounds. Spread the sun-dried tomato mixture on the meat, according to your taste preference.

CASTLE MARNE

Denver grew with the hordes of people who showed up to search for gold in the area. The discovery of the Comstock Lode in Nevada precipitated another rush of humanity to the West, all searching for their fortunes. And quite a few found them in Colorado.

New wealth was demonstrated by the construction of numerous elegant mansions around the city. The Wyman District, now recognized as a historical section of town, contained a number of these mansions. Much of the construction occurred between 1888 and 1893, and prominent architect William Lang built 36 of the houses. The area was home to many of Denver's most prominent citizens, including many members of the "Sacred 36." They were the ones fortunate enough to be invited to Mrs. Crawford Hill's bridge parties. Why 36? Because she set out nine tables.

Castle Marne was built in the Wyman area in 1889 at the height of the silver boom. It is considered by many to be one of the finest examples of the enduring style of eclectic architect William Lang, who also designed the Unsinkable Molly Brown's house. The history of Castle Marne glows through the hand-rubbed woods, the renowned circular stained-glass Peacock Window, and its original ornate fireplaces.

In past years, Castle Marne was also referred to as the Raymond House. It was originally built for William S. Raymond, who paid $15,000 for the land and $40,000 for the construction. Raymond sold the house to Colonel James H. Platt, a business associate of John D. Rockefeller and a former member of President Grant's Cabinet. In 1891, Platt built the largest and finest paper mill in the world in Denver.

Following the economic crash of 1893, when the U.S. government ceased buying vast quantities of silver, a halt occurred in most building. Silver prices plummeted, businesses and banks closed, and vast fortunes were lost. Energy in the field of construction was directed at the conversion of mansions into multi-unit apartment buildings. Through a succession of owners, Castle Marne survived and now thrives as a luxury urban inn and bed and breakfast.

A stay at Castle Marne combines Victorian charm with modern-day convenience and comfort. Each guest room is furnished with authentic period antiques, family heirlooms, and exacting reproductions to create the mood of long-ago charm and romance. Some suites come with a private outdoor hot tub.

To accentuate the mood and the old-world atmosphere, Castle Marne offers three kinds of tea. Two teas are served at 1 o'clock, and visitors are welcomed. The tea served from 4:30 to 6:00 daily is available only to "Inn-House" guests and serves as a relaxing time to make plans for dinner and meet with each other and the innkeepers at the Marne.

Castle Marne serves gourmet candlelight six-course dinners in the original formal dining room as well as full Victorian luncheons in the Castle's Parlor.

Castle Marne
1572 Race Street
Denver, Colorado 80206
(303) 331-0621
(800) 92MARNE

Castle Crab Salad

In a saucepan filled with a small amount of water, cook the asparagus covered for about 5 minutes, or until it is a crisp tender. Drain well. Add crab, corn, croutons, green pepper, red pepper, and scallions. In a separate bowl, whisk together oil, lemon juice, mustard, pepper, pepper sauce, cayenne, salt, and sugar until well blended. Toss dressing with salad. Chill well and serve.

 YIELD

Serves 8–10

8 ounces fresh asparagus,
cut into 1-inch pieces

1 pound fresh crabmeat,
shredded

14 ounces whole baby corn,
drained and rinsed

1 cup plain croutons

1 large sweet green pepper,
chopped

1 large red pepper, chopped

3 scallions with tops, chopped

DRESSING

¼ cup vegetable or olive oil

1 tablespoon lemon juice

1 tablespoon Dijon mustard

⅛ teaspoon pepper

3 drops hot red pepper sauce

1 pinch of cayenne pepper
(optional)

1 pinch salt

1 pinch sugar

4 cups packed greens,
    including spinach,
    iceberg, leaf lettuce, etc.

1 can (14.75 ounces) Alaska pink
    salmon

3 tablespoons olive oil

½ cup chopped onion

6 tablespoons nasturtium vinegar
    or red wine vinegar

2 tablespoons water

1 teaspoon sugar

2 teaspoons dried, crushed red
    chilies

1 tablespoon olive oil

2 teaspoons Dijon mustard

salt and pepper to taste

12–14 fresh nasturtium blossoms

fresh basil sprigs for garnish

Nasturtium Salmon Salad

Many varieties of edible flowers are served at the Historic Castle Marne, but the old-fashioned nasturtiums from the kitchen garden are favorites.

Place greens in large bowl and chill. Heat olive oil in skillet over medium heat; add chopped onions and sauté until translucent. Add vinegar, water, sugar, and chilies and bring to boil. Let cool. Mix olive oil and Dijon into a paste. Add to onion mixture. Add salt and pepper to taste. Add salmon chunks and stir carefully, then chill. To serve, toss with salad greens. Garnish with fresh nasturtium blossoms and basil sprigs. Enjoy!

Variation: 1 pound of spicy Italian sausage may be substituted for the salmon.

YIELD
Serves 4

Cherry Soup

This delightful chilled soup is the perfect teatime refreshment on a hot summer day. It is our innkeeper Ursula's mother's family recipe.

Boil cherries, water, and sugar in a large saucepan over high heat. Reduce heat and simmer for 15–20 minutes or until cherries are soft. In a small bowl, whisk cornstarch and cold water until smooth. Slowly add to cherry soup while stirring. Let the mixture cook a few minutes to thicken. Add almond, vanilla, and lemon juice and mix well. Remove from heat and refrigerate soup for 6 hours or overnight until thoroughly chilled. Serve in small bowls with a generous dollop of sour cream on top.

 YIELD

Makes about 8 cups

6 cups pitted sour cherries

6 cups water

1½ cups sugar or to taste

5 tablespoons cornstarch

½ cup cold water

2 teaspoons almond extract

2 teaspoons vanilla extract

2 tablespoons lemon juice
    or to taste

sour cream

Tomato Curry Soup

½ cup chopped onion

4 tablespoons butter

2½ teaspoons curry powder

28 ounces crushed tomatoes
(canned or fresh)

30 ounces chicken stock

½ cup sour cream

fresh parsley or chopped chives

Guests love this soup, and they always ask, "What is that special ingredient?"

In a large saucepan, sauté onions in butter until soft. Add curry powder and cook for another minute to blend the flavors. Add tomatoes and chicken stock. Bring to a boil and then reduce heat and simmer for 15–20 minutes. Add sour cream and let it melt in the soup. Whisk soup until smooth, or pour into a blender and puree. Garnish with a little dollop of sour cream and fresh parsley or chopped chives. At Castle Marne, we also tuck a fresh sprig of basil beside the bowl and float a fresh nasturtium blossom.

YIELD
Serves 6–8

Cranberry Tea Bread

Here's another perfect holiday treat that guests at Castle Marne ask for each year.

Preheat oven to 350 degrees. Spray a 9-by-5-inch loaf pan. In a large bowl, mix together flour, whole wheat flour, brown sugar, cinnamon, ginger, baking powder, and soda. Set aside. In a small bowl, beat together oil, eggs, orange juice, and orange rind. Stir egg mixture into flour mixture just until moistened. Stir in cranberries and chopped pecans. Spoon batter into prepared pan and bake for about 60 minutes, or until a toothpick inserted in the center comes out clean. Cool on a wire rack for 10 minutes, then remove from pan. Cool completely, slice and serve.

"Tea is an affront to lunch and an insult to dinner."

—Mark Twain

2 cups flour

½ cup whole wheat flour

1½ cups brown sugar

1 teaspoon ground cinnamon

½ teaspoon ground ginger

2 teaspoons baking powder

1 teaspoon baking soda

⅓ cup oil

2 large eggs

¾ cup orange juice

grated rind of one orange

2 cups cranberries, chopped

½ cup pecans, chopped

1 egg

⅓ cup canola oil

¾ cup eggnog

¼ cup rum

2 cups flour

1 tablespoon baking powder

½ teaspoon salt

⅔ cup sugar

1 teaspoon nutmeg for garnish

Eggnog Muffins

These muffins are a special treat during the holiday season.

Preheat oven to 350 degrees. In a small bowl, stir together egg, oil, eggnog, and rum and set aside. Sift together flour, baking powder, salt, and sugar in a medium-size bowl. Make a well in the center and add the egg mixture. Mix together just until dry ingredients are moistened. Spray mini-muffin pans. Fill the cups with the muffin batter ¾ full and sprinkle the tops with nutmeg. Bake approximately 15–20 minutes or until the tops are lightly browned.

YIELD

Makes 36 mini-muffins

THE FORT

Back in the early 1800s, when Mexico and the fledgling United States were contesting control of the West, William and Charles Bent and Ceran St. Vrain built a fort in 1833 along the then boundary with Mexico. Owned by the St. Vrain Company and situated along the thriving Santa Fe Trail between La Junta and Las Animas near Lamar, the fort was designed and strategically located to expand the company's trading empire. Bent's Fort, as it was called, attracted Native Americans and trappers who traveled there to trade goods.

The fort was the only major permanent white settlement on the Santa Fe Trail between the Mississippi River and Mexico. Travelers on the trail would stop there for supplies, wagon repair, livestock, and good food and water as well as for rest and company. When the Mexican War erupted in 1846, the fort served as a staging ground for Colonel Stephen Watts Kearney's "Army of the West." In 1849, and after the United States had won the war, the fort was abandoned. This was partially due to disease and disaster, but also reflected the fact that the war was over, and most able-bodied folks were headed for the California gold fields.

Samuel P. Arnold had worked in advertising and as a toy salesman, but he always maintained his appreciation for history and was a lover of good food. While browsing through historical photographs at Denver's public library in 1962, he discovered some drawings of Bent's Fort. Inspired by this 1830s fur trading and freighting center on the Santa Fe Trail, Sam decided to build a home that looked like the fort.

Arnold found a scenic seven-acre plot of land high on the hill with Denver's lights twinkling below. Pikes Peak was visible 70 miles away. It was the perfect spot for his home to be built, but banks refused him a residential loan. Arnold quickly decided to open a restaurant on the first floor of his fort, just to secure a business construction loan from the Small Business Administration.

Arnold hired a 25-man crew from Taos to build the structure, using 80,000 forty-five-pound adobe bricks (each made on the site), supported by hand-hewn beams. The floors were made the same color as the original "blood floors" of the period. The St. Vrain Bar floor was made in the traditional mixture of earth and ox blood, but is now visible only under the wood planks since ladies' high heels and earthen floors are incompatible.

Sam Arnold first focused his attention on opening the downstairs restaurant. True to his dream, Arnold immersed himself in the world of Bent's Fort. To create an environment that would reflect the 1830s and 1840s in every way possible, he researched the foods that were served at the fort and along the Santa Fe Trail—buffalo, peppers, and gunpowder whiskey.

Sam enjoyed cooking all his life. While a teenager at Andover Academy (where George Herbert Walker Bush went to school and met Barbara), Arnold treated schoolmates to late-night fried eggs and bacon sandwiches. However, running a restaurant was a whole new challenge. Even his hired chefs were overwhelmed when they ran out of food in 2 hours on Thanksgiving Day, while 300 customers waited.

Arnold injected himself into the kitchen in an effort to avoid further embarrassment. This experience inspired him to study cooking with James Beard and culinary skills at La Varenne Ecole de Cuisine in Paris. He also attended cooking classes in Sri Lanka, Thailand, and the People's Republic of China. His attention to detail has encouraged trips to ranches, farms, and groves, all in search of the products he wished to serve.

Sam Arnold's original vision of 1962 is a reality. Visitors are immediately reminded of history as they enter The Fort's courtyard through massive doors. The rock firepit glows, and an Indian tepee reminds everyone that Bent's Fort was a licensed trading center for the many Indian tribes that inhabited the area as well as fur traders and pioneers moving west and south. On occasion, a military band of the period might be playing on the balcony.

There are nine unique dining rooms, each with its own beehive fireplace. The city of Denver sprawls below the windows of the dining room as well as the patio. As a holiday treat, guests will see *farolitos* (candle lights in paper bags) placed along the walls of The Fort and along the courtyard walkways.

Arnold's pioneer spirit has been the inspiration for The Fort's menu. He researched more than 2,000 books and diaries kept by trappers and traders along the 19th-century Santa Fe Trail to turn his restaurant into a historical culinary experience. The Fort serves more than 50,000 buffalo dinners annually, and not just in the form of steaks or prime rib. The menu also boasts buffalo hump, tongue, sausage, and "Rocky Mountain Oysters" as well as salmon, beef, pintade or guinea hen, elk, Colorado lamb, and many other exceptional entrees.

Sam Arnold's philosophy has always been to give his guests "shinin' times." "When people walk in with a cape of woes, miseries, frustrations and angers," says Arnold, "we want to take them away to another place, with time out from life, to restore and refresh their spirits." Step into the world of mountain men as you repeat their toast with him: "Here's to the childs what come afore, and here's to the pilgrims what's come arter. May yer trails be free of grizzlies, your packs filled with plews, and may you have fat buffler in your pot. WAUGH!"

The Fort
19192 Highway 8
Morrison, Colorado 80465
(303) 697-4771

26

1 can (12 ounces) pickled
  jalapeno peppers

1½ cups peanut butter
  (smooth or chunky)

Jalapenos Stuffed with Peanut Butter

Lucy Delgado, well known in the 1960s as a traditionalist New Mexican cook, taught me this recipe. "These are the best appetizers I know," she said. "But if I show you how to make them, you have to promise to try them." They sounded stranger than a five-legged buffalo, but I vowed to taste them. When they were ready, Lucy's last words of instruction were "Pop the entire pepper into your mouth so you're not left with a mouthful of hot jalapeno and too little peanut butter." I gamely took the little morsel by the stem and in it went. Miracle! Delicious!

Fearful of serving them to guests but eager to try them out on friends, I made them for my own parties until they became so popular that I put them on the menu. When NBC's Today *show came to Denver, Bryant Gumbel ate eight of them in a row. (Jane Pauley would have none of it).*

Slice the pickled jalapenos in half lengthwise not quite all the way through, leaving the two halves attached at the stem end. Using a knife or spoon, remove the seeds and ribs under running water. Fill each jalapeno with peanut butter.

Pack the plate. Be sure to warn guests to put the whole pepper (except the stem) in the mouth before chewing, to get 70% peanut butter and 30% jalapeno. A nibbler squeezes out the peanut butter, changing the percentages and making it very hot indeed.

Note: A fun variation is to mix Major Grey's chutney with the peanut butter. It gives a nice fruity sweetness that also buffers the burn.

3 green Anaheim chilies, roasted
    and peeled (canned will do,
    but fresh are best)

salt

1 clove garlic, chopped

1 pinch of Mexican leaf oregano

1 thick-cut New York strip, top
    sirloin, tenderloin, or buffalo
    steak (10–12 ounces)

½ teaspoon salad oil

freshly ground black pepper

1 teaspoon butter (optional)

Gonzales Steak

Slit the chilies to remove the seeds. Chop two chilies into fine dice and mix with the salt, garlic, and oregano. (New Mexicans traditionally like to leave a few of the seeds in the dish. The seeds give it life, they say).

With a very sharp knife, cut a horizontal pocket into the steak. Stuff the chopped chilies into the pocket. Brush the meat and the remaining chili with salad oil. Grill the steak on both sides to the desired doneness. If using buffalo, watch carefully so as not to overcook! Because it contains less fat than chicken, bison cooks much faster than beef and is best medium rare.

Salt and pepper the meat. Grill the remaining whole roasted chili to get a nice patterning of grid burn on it. Lay it across the steak as a garnish. A teaspoon of brown butter on the steak as a special treat is heaven. To make brown butter, simply place the butter in a sauté pan over medium-high heat and allow it to melt and turn golden brown.

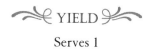

YIELD

Serves 1

Triple-Cherry Cast Iron Cobbler

Preheat oven to 375 degrees. In electric mixer, combine all dry ingredients, except butter, at low speed. Slowly add a couple of cubes of butter at a time until it is all used. Mix until streusel becomes crumbly. Keep cold until use.

To make cobbler, mix cherry juice, nectar, sugar, and salt together in a medium saucepan on stove. When mixture comes to boil, add cornstarch liquid and turn heat down to low/medium. Cook juice 3–5 minutes, stirring constantly.

Place cherries in 1-quart cast iron kettle or baking dish and pour thickened juice mixture over them. Cover with streusel and bake for at least 30 minutes until golden brown. Let sit 30 minutes and serve.

Note: This cobbler goes great with vanilla ice cream.

YIELD
Serves 4–8

FILLING

1 can (12–14 ounces) pitted bing cherries (Strain and save juice.)

1 cup sun-dried cherries

1 can (12–14 ounces) pitted, tart cherries (Not pie filling; save juice.)

⅓ cup sugar

½ cup apricot nectar

½ teaspoon salt

¼ cup cornstarch mixed with water to a thin paste

STREUSEL

¾ stick cold butter, cut into cubes

1 cup all-purpose flour

1 cup quick-cooking oats

¼ cup slivered almonds (untoasted)

1¼ cup packed brown sugar

½ teaspoon cinnamon

HOTEL TEATRO

As Denver grew into a city, it developed a need for public transportation, and the Denver Electric and Cable Company was incorporated in 1885. The following year, it changed its name to the Denver Tramway Company, which was quite unusual in America. Very few city systems referred to themselves as tramways, although the term was very common in Europe.

As operations expanded, the Tramway Company built a new headquarters in 1911. This site had also been the location of the Evans Mansion, which was the home of John Evans, Colorado's second territorial governor. John's oldest son, W. G. Evans, had become president of the Denver Tramway Company, and he decided the firm needed an eight-story office tower and adjacent three-story car barn.

The building's design combined a modern steel skeleton and Chicago style office space with a traditional Renaissance Revival style edifice of glazed red brick and glazed white terra-cotta. This same style was carried into the lobby, where the use of Tennessee light pink marble flooring and Vermont green marble base were combined with white Arizona marble wainscoting. The elegance of the original office building, which has since become the Hotel Teatro, can be seen today in the entrance to the hotel as careful attention was paid to preserve this detail.

Following WWII, transportation by streetcar became obsolete in Denver. The University of Colorado at Denver took advantage of the opportunity and purchased the Tramway Building, making it the nucleus of its downtown campus. The school faculty moved into the Tramway offices, and the area where trolleys once parked was converted into classrooms.

By the late 1980s, The University of Colorado at Denver had moved all of its facilities across Cherry Creek to the Auraria Campus. In 1991, the Denver Center for the Performing Arts purchased the car barn portion of the building for the offices, workshop, and storage area. The tower part of the Tramway Building remained vacant for several more years.

In 1997, Astonbridge Partners hired David Owen Tyrba Architects to transform and restore the Tramway Building into the luxury hotel that stands today. The immediate proximity to the Performing Arts Complex was the inspiration for the name *Teatro*, which means "theatre" in Italian. Hotel Teatro is designed to blend the grandeur of old Colorado with the modern conveniences available today.

Hotel Teatro is located in the heart of downtown Denver, directly across from the Denver Center for Performing Arts and just two blocks from the Colorado Convention Center. The 16th Street Mall, Larimer Square, and the nightlife of the Lower Downtown ("LoDo") Historic District are only steps from the front door. Coors Field, the Pepsi Center, and Denver Pavilions are also within walking distance. The majestic backdrop of the Colorado Rocky Mountains and the central Denver location makes Hotel Teatro an excellent choice for business or pleasure.

Hotel Teatro
1100 14th Street
Denver, Colorado 80202
(303) 228-1100

5 cups heavy cream

1¾ cups sugar

1 vanilla bean, sliced open

10 sheets gelatin

7 cups buttermilk

1 whole pineapple, cored and
    cut into ¼-inch cubes

2 cups sugar

Hawaiian Pineapple Charlotte
with Buttermilk Panna Cotta

Bring the cream, sugar, and vanilla bean to a boil. Add gelatin to above mixture, stirring until dissolved. Add the buttermilk. Pour into ring molds.

Pour sugar onto a large sheet pan. Add pineapple cubes, stirring to cover with the sugar. Roast at 400 degrees until caramelized, stirring occasionally. Cool.

Place roasted pineapple cubes in ring molds on top of the cream mixture. Refrigerate until set and serve with a cassis or raspberry sorbet.

YIELD

Makes 4–8 depending on size of ring mold

Chilled Maine Lobster Salad
with Heirloom Tomatoes, Pink Grapefruit, Spanish Almonds, and Vanilla Yogurt

Toss the heirloom tomatoes, ginger, and basil in a small mixing bowl. Season with salt and pepper and refrigerate.

In a separate mixing bowl, combine yogurt, lime juice, and vanilla; refrigerate.

To assemble, spoon the heirloom tomato salad in the center of a medium salad plate. Place the lobster tail on the tomatoes. Fan three grapefruit segments at the bottom of the plate and garnish the lobster tail with four Spanish almonds. Spoon the vanilla yogurt around the tomatoes and garnish with micro greens on top of the almonds.

YIELD
Serves 4

4 half lobster tails (season with salt and pepper, poach in butter, shell and chill)

2 heirloom tomatoes, diced small

1 teaspoon fresh ginger

2 basil leaves

1 grapefruit (segmented, approximately 16 pieces)

16 Spanish almonds

½ cup plain yogurt

1 lime

½ vanilla bean

salt and pepper to taste

micro greens to garnish

1 package goat cheese

1 red pepper (seeded, roasted, and peeled)

1 bunch fresh arugula

OLIVE TAPENADE

½ cup delicatessen-style black olives

1 white anchovy

1 small clove of garlic

¼ teaspoon lemon zest

2 ounces olive oil

2 fresh basil leaves

kalamata olives for tapenade

smoked Spanish paprika (pimienton)

fennel seeds, whole

poppy seeds, whole

salt and pepper

extra virgin olive oil

Prima Ristorante Denver Goat Cheese Truffles
with Arugula and Roasted Red Pepper Salad and Olive Tapenade

Cut one red pepper in half, remove seeds, place with skin side up, and roast until the skin is blackened. Discard skin and slice into strips.

OLIVE TAPENADE

Combine olives, anchovy, garlic, lemon zest, olive oil, and basil leaves; puree. Season with salt and pepper to taste.

Remove stems from the fresh arugula for the salad. Create truffle-sized balls with the goat cheese (12 total).

In three small bowls, prepare the following:

poppy seeds
fennel seeds
Spanish paprika (a.k.a. pimienton)

Chill four salad-sized plates. Roll four goat cheese balls in each of the three bowls and place directly on plates to serve. Place a small portion of arugula on each plate and arrange the sliced red peppers on the arugula. Drizzle with olive oil and add salt and pepper to taste. Decorate plate and arugula with olive tapenade.

YIELD

Serves 4

Seared Diver Scallops
with Saffron Risotto and Green Asparagus

Sauté shallots and garlic until translucent. Add rice and coat in oil. Add white wine slowly, then saffron. Next add vegetable stock and cook until rice is tender. Add cheese and butter and mix until tender. Season with salt and pepper.

Trim 12 spears of asparagus and blanch in boiling, salted water for 90 seconds. Sauté in hot olive oil for 90 seconds and season with salt and pepper.

Coat sauté pan with olive oil and bring to high heat. Salt and pepper the scallops and place in hot pan. Sear on both sides for 2 minutes.

Lightly drizzle plate with olive oil and aged balsamic.

YIELD
Serves 4

12 scallops (8 per pound), cleaned

1 large shallot

2 garlic cloves

1 cup Arborio rice

1½ cups dry white wine

1 pinch saffron

2 cups hot vegetable stock

½ cup Parmesan cheese

½ pound salted butter

salt and pepper

12 asparagus spears

olive oil

salt and pepper

OXFORD HOTEL

When gold was discovered at Sutter's Mill in California in 1849, the rush of miners to the west in 1849 set the stage for the development of modern Colorado. While the Cliff Dwellers and Mexican explorers occupied much of modern-day Colorado for a thousand years or more, the real influx of Americans resulted from the winning of the Mexican American War in 1848, and the discovery of small amounts of gold near the confluence of the South Platte River and Cherry Creek.

In 1806, Lieutenant Zebulon M. Pike and a small party of U.S. soldiers had been sent to explore the southwestern boundary of the Louisiana Purchase. They discovered the peak that bears the lieutenant's name, but failed in effort to climb it. When word got out that gold had been discovered in the Colorado frontier, which was then part of Kansas Territory, tens of thousands of miners, speculators, and businessmen (both honest and dishonest) flocked to Colorado. Their cry was "Pike's Peak or Bust."

Enough people arrived in Colorado to create a number of towns and a territorial government. While searching for gold, miners discovered vast quantities of silver mixed with lead carbonate ores near present-day Leadville, which brought more people and formal statehood for Colorado in 1876.

By 1890, Denver had grown to be the third largest city in the West. Riding the crest of the great wealth that came from silver mining, and the thirst of miners for beer, Phil Zang built a brewing empire that rivaled the one he had sold in Louisville, Kentucky. Phil sold his interests in 1888 and turned management of the brewery over to his son, Adolph. It was Adolph's vision that Denver needed a grand hotel, and he financed the building of the Oxford Hotel in 1891. The architect, Frank E. Edbrooke, also designed The Brown Palace Hotel, which was erected a year after the Oxford Hotel, making the Oxford the oldest downtown hotel in Denver.

The vast quantities of gold found in California and Colorado had to this point created national wealth in the form of officially minted gold coins. When silver became plentiful, its price per ounce declined. In 1890, President Benjamin Harrison tried to solve this problem and had Congress pass the Sherman Silver Purchase Act. The government agreed to purchase $4.5 million ounces of silver a month to raise prices. The price of silver nearly doubled overnight from 84 cents to $1.50 an ounce and treasury silver notes were issued that could be exchanged for silver or gold.

By 1893, so many silver notes had been exchanged for real gold that the government's coffers were all but empty. The act was repealed that year, causing the greatest economic panic the nation had ever seen. Silver mines closed along with most of the banks that backed them, and many of the businesses that supported mining and its infrastructure also closed. But the Oxford Hotel not only survived, it became a small city within the city.

The Oxford had its own restaurant, barber shop, library, pharmacy, Western Union office, horse stables, and saloon, all of which served Zang's beer. There was little need for people to go anywhere else.

The Oxford was located near Union Station, so trains brought many guests almost to the hotel's front door. The war years saw many troop trains arriving in Denver, which helped to keep business brisk. After WWII, tourism helped keep business going, but the decline in train travel eventually caused the hotel to close for a period. Completely renovated and restored to its original grandeur, the hotel was reopened in 1983. The Oxford Hotel is an original landmark from Denver's colorful history. McCormick's Fish House & Bar in the hotel is a popular downtown eatery.

The Oxford Hotel
1600 17th Street
Denver, Colorado 80202
(303) 628-5400

CURRY BASE

3 tablespoons vegetable oil

5 tablespoons red curry paste

2 cups canned coconut milk

MUSSELS

2 tablespoons clarified butter

2 tablespoons garlic, chopped

2 shallots, chopped

20 ounces black mussels

½ cup Roma tomatoes,
    diced to about ½ inch

½ cup chicken stock

1½ cups prepared curry base
    (recipe above)

1 tablespoon freshly squeezed
    lime juice

Steamed Mussels in Red Curry Sauce

A little spicy, a little sweet, and a little rich, these mussels are a lot delicious! As a bonus, they are quick and easy!

CURRY BASE

To prepare the curry base, sauté the curry paste in hot oil. Add the coconut milk and bring to a boil. Set aside.

MUSSELS

Sauté the garlic and shallots in the butter. Add the mussels and tomatoes. Toss well. Add the chicken stock, curry base, and lime juice. Cover and steam until the mussels are open. Pour mussels into bowls and arrange them with the open ends facing up.

YIELD

Serves 2

Niçoise Salad

This salad originated in Nice, France. It was prepared with processed, canned tuna; but using great fresh ahi and searing it briefly gives it a contemporary spin. It makes a perfect lunch any time of the year, but when the local tomatoes are fresh, it's at its best.

2 red potatoes, halved and cooked

½ cup diced, mixed tomatoes

1 ounce green beans, blanched

6 kalamata olives, pitted

1 boiled egg, quartered

½ ounce basil oil

½ ounce extra virgin olive oil

3 ounces ahi tuna, sliced

¼ ounce micro greens (optional)

Place the potato halves in the center of the plate. Toss the tomato salad, olives, and beans together with the oils. Place this mixture on top of the potatoes. Sear the tuna for a few seconds on each side, and slice. Place sliced tuna on top of the salad. Place the quartered egg on each end of the plate. Top with micro greens if desired.

 YIELD

Serves 1

"Denver's population is the thinnest of any city in the U.S. . . . Less than 20% of its adults are overweight."

—Federal Study

4 salmon fillets (5 ounces each;
not steaks)

6 ounces Dungeness crabmeat

6 ounces bay shrimp

6 ounces brie, cut into
½-inch cubes

3 tablespoons mayonnaise

1 tablespoon fresh dill, chopped

1 pinch of salt

1 pinch of pepper

BEURRE BLANC

6 ounces white wine

3 ounces white wine vinegar

3 whole black peppercorns

1 shallot, quartered

1 cup heavy cream

6 ounces cold, unsalted butter,
cut into pieces

Stuffed Salmon with Crab and Shrimp
with Beurre Blanc Sauce

While dining at McCormick and Schmick's in Portland, Oregon, Bill McCormick once called this dish "one of the most perfect meals I've ever had." For all its glory, it's easy to prepare—just a few ingredients blended together perfectly.

Combine wine, vinegar, peppercorns, and shallot in a noncorrosive saucepan (stainless steel, Teflon, Calphalon). Reduce until the mixture totals just 1 to 2 tablespoons and has the consistency of syrup. Add the cream and reduce again until the mixture totals 3 to 4 tablespoons and is very syrupy.

Remove the pan from heat. Add the butter pieces, about 2 ounces at a time, stirring constantly and allowing each piece to melt in before adding more. (If the mixture cools too much, the butter will not melt completely and you will have to reheat it slightly.) Strain and hold warm on a stovetop trivet or in a double boiler over very low heat until you are ready to use. Makes 1 cup.

Preheat oven to 400 degrees. Prepare the beurre blanc sauce and set aside. Split the halibut fillets lengthwise to form a pocket for the stuffing. Combine the crab, shrimp, brie, dill, salt, and pepper. Gently blend in the mayonnaise to bind the mixture. Divide the stuffing mixture between the four pocketed fillets. When full, let the flaps cover the stuffing so that only a small amount is exposed. Bake in a lightly buttered baking dish for 10 to 12 minutes. Transfer to dinner plates and spoon the beurre blanc over the fish.

YIELD

Serves 4

PANZANO

The city of Denver began as a mining camp during the Colorado gold rush. Although most history records the Colorado gold rush as having occurred in 1859, it really began for a few in late 1858. William Russell and several other prospectors had set up camp at the confluence of Cherry Creek and the South Platte River; they called their settlement Auraria. Just before the winter began, Russell discovered gold on this site, which is near present downtown Denver.

Word got out quickly, and most people made plans for an early spring rush into what was then called western Kansas Territory. One of the few hardy souls who got there early was General William Larimer. Having earned his rank in the Pennsylvania Militia, Larimer was a railroad man and land speculator in Kansas. On the way to the new gold fields, his group joined forces with another, which included E. W. "Ned" Wynkoop.

The combined groups reached Russell's campsite, Auraria, in November 1858, and Larimer laid claim to a square mile of the hillside across the river on the higher ground. Many people credit the general with having given the name to the city of Denver; but some believe that Ned Wynkoop, who had been appointed sheriff of Arapahoe County, actually suggested that it be named after James Denver, the new governor of the western territory.

The new community flourished, along with the great influx of prospectors and miners in the spring of 1859. Eventually, Denver grew to incorporate Auraria and all the surrounding communities. Today, it is the largest city in the state. With an official elevation of precisely 5,280 feet, it is routinely referred to as "the Mile High City."

Located in the heart of Denver's central business district, the Hotel Monaco Denver offers easy access to the 16th Street Mall and Lower Downtown (or LoDo, as the residents of Denver affectionately call it). LoDo includes Larimer Square, the place where Denver City was actually founded. The square today is filled with art galleries, shops, cafés, restaurants, and brew pubs. LoDo also contains Coors Field, just down the street, and Denver's Colorado Convention Center, only four blocks away from Hotel Monaco. Three blocks further is Denver's U.S. Mint.

The 23-square-block area of LoDo marks the true origin of the city. The neighborhood was declared a historic district in 1988 and today gives protection to over 100 historic buildings. The 16th Street Mall is a European-style pedestrian district. Trees now stand where cars used to run along this 16-block promenade that forms the heart of downtown Denver. The 16th Street Mall features fine restaurants, cafés and bars, plus outstanding shopping.

Hotel Monaco Denver is a luxury boutique hotel offering an exceptional restaurant in Panzano. Visit the capital of Colorado and enjoy a great meal at the Hotel Monaco.

Panzano

909 Seventeenth Street

Denver, Colorado 80202

(303) 296-3525

Mushroom Crepes
with Fonduta Sauce

MUSHROOM FILLING

1 cup wild mushroom mix,
    sliced ¼ inch thick

2 teaspoons garlic, chopped

2 teaspoons fresh thyme, chopped

1 teaspoon sea salt

1 tablespoon unsalted butter

1 tablespoon olive oil

FONDUTA SAUCE

1 tablespoon olive oil

1 cup heavy cream

½ cup diced shallots

1 teaspoon chopped garlic

¼ cup white wine

¼ cup chicken stock

1 ounce Fontina, grated

1 ounce Gorgonzola, grated

1 ounce Parmesan, grated

CREPES

½ cup flour

1 egg

⅔ cup milk

1 tablespoon butter, melted

4 teaspoons white truffle oil

MUSHROOM FILLING

Heat sauté pan; add butter and olive oil. Add mushrooms, garlic, and thyme. Once they are tender, add salt. Then place a small portion in a crepe. Roll up and set seam side down.

FONDUTA SAUCE

Heat olive oil. Add shallots and garlic. Cook on a low temperature or flame. Once the vegetables are translucent, add wine and chicken stock. Reduce by half. Add cream. Heat to a boil. Slowly add the cheese until all is incorporated. Reduce sauce until slightly thickened.

CREPES

Make crepes first. Combine all ingredients. Allow to rest for 1 hour. Spray a nonstick crepe or egg pan with oil. Take a 2-ounce ladle and pour the batter into the pan. Roll the batter around until it creates a perfect circle. Let it cook until you see the edges curl and the crepe slides around freely. Then flip to quickly set the other side. Then place on plate, layering the crepes like shingles as you go.

To assemble the crepes, heat a sauté pan again with a little olive oil. Sear your crepes seam side down first. Then flip and toast the other side. Place on a plate and pour fonduta sauce over the top.

Lastly, drizzle white truffle oil over the crepes and serve. Enjoy.

YIELD

Serves 4

4 ounces Bolognese sauce

2 ounces cinnamon custard
(recipe follows)

2 tablespoons Parmesan, grated

4 ounces pappardelle pasta

CINNAMON CUSTARD

½ cup granulated sugar

6 inches of cinnamon stick

2 cups milk

3 large eggs

Bolognese al Forno

Heat Bolognese sauce. Cook pasta.

Toss the pasta with the Bolognese sauce. Place in bowls. Drizzle custard around the rim of the pasta. Top with grated Parmesan and bake until cheese is golden. Top with chopped parsley.

CINNAMON CUSTARD

In a saucepan, combine sugar and cinnamon with milk and bring to a boil. Remove from heat, cool slightly, and cover. Refrigerate at least 8 hours.

After chilling, preheat the oven to 325 degrees. Reheat the milk mixture in a saucepan to a scald and remove cinnamon stick.

In a bowl, beat eggs, then add milk mixture slowly, beating as you pour. Fill six 5-ounce custard cups. Set in shallow pan on oven rack. Pour hot water into pan 1 inch deep. Bake at 325 degrees for 40 to 45 minutes, or until knife inserted comes out clean. Serve warm or chilled.

For one large custard, bake in 1-quart casserole about 60 minutes.

ROCKY MOUNTAIN DINER

There was gold in the hills of Colorado, and that is what first attracted miners and prospectors to the area. But it was the discovery of silver in Leadville in 1875 that really boosted the local economy and drew tens of thousands of people to the territory.

As Denver grew in prominence and size from all the new residents, and as silver mining became the new path to extravagant wealth, many elegant homes were built by the new rich. The popular Denver architect William Lang was credited with building dozens of homes and several commercial buildings. The only surviving commercial structure by Lang is the now famous and historic Ghost Building.

Lang and his partner Marshall Pugh were also credited with many other architectural achievements in Denver around 1890. Their firm designed the Molly Brown House, the Castle Marne, and St. Marks Church at 12th and Lincoln. St. Marks now houses a unique nightclub, appropriately called "The Church."

Originally built in 1891 at another location, the Ghost Building is one of downtown Denver's most interesting structures. It is a Romanesque style low-rise first constructed for early Colorado pioneer A. M. Ghost. For 85 years the Ghost Building stood at the corner of 14th Street and Glenarm. In 1979, the landowners decided to erect a parking lot there, so the building was dismantled, brick by brick, and moved from its original location. From there it went into storage for 10 years.

Using an elaborate system of numbering the blocks, workmen moved the 1,495 pieces of North Dakota sandstone out of storage in 1984 and reassembled them at the corner of 18th and Stout Streets. The Ghost Building now sits across from the old U.S. Post Office, a white marble structure in neoclassical design that has been renovated to house the United States Tenth Circuit Court of Appeals. Both the U.S. Post Office Building and the Ghost Building retain a graceful style and architectural elegance that is an important part of the city's history, particularly when juxtaposed among the modern steel and glass high-rises in the downtown area.

The Rocky Mountain Diner was opened in 1990 in the Ghost Building. This Western-style classic diner has been serving great portions of homespun food since then. Popular dishes include such items as buffalo meat loaf, chicken-fried steak, and turkey breast along with a selection of Mexican offerings. Don't order the buffalo meat loaf unless you are very hungry, or plan on using a doggie bag (although you won't want to share this with the dog). The restaurant also offers the largest selection of bourbon in Denver. And if your tastes in adult beverages are different, there are five brews on tap as well as a moderately priced wine list.

Rocky Mountain Diner
800 18th Street
Denver, Colorado 80202
(303) 293-8383

Duck Enchiladas

Heat duck in a skillet, being careful to not overcook. Place shredded Havarti cheese on top of duck and cover skillet to melt cheese. Transfer mixture to the pre-softened tortillas and wrap. Place tortillas on plate and ladle tomatillo-chipotle sauce around them. Spoon on the warmed black beans, red chili rice, and corn salsa. Garnish with sour cream and scallions.

TOMATILLO-CHIPOTLE SAUCE

Broil tomatillos; sauté onions, garlic, and chipotle with butter. Transfer all ingredients to a food processor. Place remaining ingredients in food processor and puree until smooth (water may be added to thin sauce). Add salt to taste if needed.

"The only real stumbling block is fear of failure. In cooking you've got to have a what-the-hell attitude."

—Julia Child

2 corn tortillas, dipped in hot oil to soften

3 ounces roasted duck breast, julienned

4 ounces Havarti cheese, shredded

3 ounces tomatillo-chipotle sauce (recipe follows)

2 ounces black beans

2 ounces red chili rice

2 ounces roasted corn salsa

1 ounce sour cream

scallions

TOMATILLO-CHIPOTLE SAUCE

1 pound tomatillos

1 tablespoon garlic, minced

1 tablespoon butter

1 onion, medium sized

2 chipotle chili peppers

6 ounces barbecue sauce

juice of 1 lime

1 teaspoon salt

2 pounds ground buffalo

1 egg

1½ ounces bread crumbs

⅓ cup milk

⅓ cup margarine (or butter)

1 cup onions, diced ¼ inch

⅓ cup celery, diced ¼ inch

1 teaspoon thyme

1 teaspoon salt

1 teaspoon black pepper

1 teaspoon garlic powder

Buffalo Meat Loaf

Combine the egg, bread crumbs, and milk. Sauté the onions and celery in the margarine until they are soft.

Combine all ingredients in a mixing bowl with a dough hook until thoroughly mixed. Do not overmix, or it will become tough!

Form into a loaf and place in a cooking pan. Bake in oven at 300 degrees until the meat reaches an internal temperature of 160 degrees.

YIELD
Serves 6–8

White Chocolate Banana Cream Pie

Toss (mix) together bananas and pineapple juice; drain. Layer in bottom of crust (single layer). Prepare the custard.

CUSTARD

Bring milk almost to a boil in kettle. Add margarine. Mix sugar and cornstarch in a bowl with a whisk. Add salt, eggs, and vanilla to bowl and whisk until smooth. When milk is hot, add half of it to the bowl, whisk to dissolve and return all to kettle. Whisk until very smooth. Cool in ice bath until mixture reaches 50 degrees. Smooth top of custard and then refrigerate for 24 hours.

When the custard has cooled, pour it into the pie crust, covering the bananas. Top with whipped cream. Sprinkle topping on pie.

TOPPING

Combine sugar, white chocolate, and cocoa powder. Sprinkle on top of pie.

YIELD
Serves 8

---

1 prebaked pie crust (larger tin; crust lightly golden)

2 medium bananas, peeled, sliced ¼ inch thick

1 tablespoon pineapple juice

1 can whipped cream

CUSTARD

2 cups milk

2 tablespoons margarine

¾ cup sugar

3 tablespoons cornstarch

¼ teaspoon salt

1 teaspoon vanilla

3 eggs

TOPPING

¼ cup sugar

4 ounces white chocolate, finely chopped

½ teaspoon cocoa powder

STRINGS RESTAURANT

Although the Southern Arapaho Indians had discovered the Denver area long before white settlers arrived, they gladly welcomed the miners and prospectors who came with the gold rush in 1859. The Indians referred to the settlers as the "spider people" because of the network of roads, fences, and survey lines they laid down as they moved through the area. The excitement of trading various pelts and furs (called "hairy bank notes") for unusual items common to the white man's world wore off rather quickly.

The confluence of the South Platte River and Cherry Creek was the site of the first gold strike. It did not take long for large numbers of prospectors and miners to arrive. Camps were established and turned into a town, which grew in size with more fortune seekers. Eventually, the town was given the name *Denver* by the local sheriff—in honor of James W. Denver, who as the governor of Kansas Territory had appointed the sheriff. At the time, eastern Colorado was under the administration of Kansas Territory.

More gold brought more people. And more people eventually discovered silver. Silver brought even more hordes of people and the railroads to support them. Then the railroads helped the population to explode as Denver grew into a city of over 100,000 people by 1890.

There was so much silver being taken out of the hills of Colorado that the United States Congress in 1890 passed the Sherman Silver Purchase Act, agreeing to buy $4.5 million of silver every month, to be exchanged for silver certificates. There was such confidence in the value of these two precious metals that the government agreed to take silver-backed money and exchange it for real gold. Little did they realize how quickly the nation's gold reserves would be depleted. The system collapsed in 1893, and the nation suffered a major economic depression when the Sherman Silver Purchase Act was repealed just to save the little remaining gold the government had.

But silver wealth was being spent at a rapid pace. So many mansions were built in Denver that they had to move outward from the center of town. One area populated by many of the city's wealthy was Uptown. A residential area east of downtown, Uptown was built up the sides of the hills. The higher up one went, the more of the city of Denver could be seen. Brown's Bluff to the west was named after Harry Brown, the owner of The Brown Palace Hotel. To the east was Swallow Hill, developed by George Ransom Swallow, the real estate and banking magnate.

Even as the silver crash hit in 1893, Uptown was nearly completely developed. In 1910, Gigantic Cleaners was opened in Uptown by the Orlin family. It operated for years until it was replaced by a New York style deli. After a period of time as a Chinese restaurant, it became Café Roncettis. More recently, this building has been the home of Strings Restaurant. The old deli area is now the pantry for Strings.

As one of Denver's hippest places to eat, Strings has entertained such notables as President Bill Clinton, Robert Redford, Francis Ford Coppola, Joan Collins, Paul McCartney, Mick Jagger, Bon Jovi, Mario Andretti, the Moscow Circus, and Michael Jordan. Linda Evans held her cast party for "Legends" at Strings.

Strings is a popular place, bustling with excitement. The dress code ranges from blue jeans to tuxedos, and the menu focuses on new American cuisine.

Strings Restaurant
1700 Humboldt Street
Denver, Colorado 80218
(303) 831-7310

Noel Cunningham's Chocolate Soufflé

SOUFFLÉ CUPS

1 ounce butter

2 ounces sugar for soufflé cups

SAUCE

2 cups white sugar

2 ounces brown sugar

½ ounce instant espresso

2½ ounces ground chocolate

SOUFFLÉ MIX

2 cups milk

1½ ounces brown sugar

2½ ounces Ghirardelli ground chocolate

1 ounce flour + 1 ounce butter, mixed to a paste

8 egg whites

½ ounce instant espresso

SOUFFLÉ CUPS

Butter the inside of the cups and then coat them with sugar.

SAUCE

Mix all ingredients; bring to a boil and simmer for 3 minutes.

Transfer into a small pitcher to pour into the soufflés.

SOUFFLÉ MIX

Bring milk, sugar, espresso, and chocolate to a boil. Whisk in flour and butter paste. Cook for 4 minutes.

Beat egg whites until stiff. Add the soufflé mix, folding gently into the whites.

Place the mix into 8 soufflé cups. Place the cups on a baking sheet with a layer of water in it. Bake at 400 degrees for 10 minutes.

Make a hole in the middle with an inverted spoon. Pour the sauce into the hole and serve immediately.

 YIELD

Serves 8

Strings Penne Bagutta

In a large sauté pan, melt butter over medium-high heat. Add chicken and allow to brown on all sides. Add garlic, mushrooms, and tomatoes. Continue to sauté until garlic starts to brown.

Add tomato sauce, cream, and chili flakes. Lower heat to medium and reduce by one-third. Add cooked penne pasta. Season with salt and pepper. Finish with Parmesan and parsley. Garnish with steamed broccoli florets.

 YIELD

Serves 4

"No mean woman can cook well, for it calls for a light head, a generous spirit and a large heart."

—Paul Gaugin

2 cups heavy cream

2 cups tomato sauce

10 medium white mushrooms, sliced

2 large chicken breasts, cleaned, chopped into ½-inch pieces

3 ounces unsalted butter

2 tablespoons fresh parsley, chopped

2 Roma tomatoes, peeled, seeded, and coarsely chopped

red chili flakes to taste

salt and pepper to taste

½ cup grated Parmesan cheese

12 broccoli florets, steamed 3 minutes

1 teaspoon minced garlic

1 pound penne (or other) pasta

1 cup clarified butter

12 Roma tomatoes, cored

12 red bell peppers,
    seeded and chopped

1 stalk of celery, chopped

2 small yellow onions, chopped

2 carrots, chopped

½ cup minced garlic

1 gallon chicken broth

¾ gallon water

½ gallon heavy cream

1 ounce chicken bouillon
    (we recommend the "Better
    than Bouillon" brand)

salt and pepper to taste

Strings Roasted Tomato and Red Pepper Bisque

In a large pot, heat the clarified butter. (*Clarified* means having all the butter solids removed. You can achieve this by slowly heating the butter and removing the white foam that rises to the top. Do this until you have a clear liquid. You can use oil if time is an issue, but butter is better.)

After heating the butter, add the next six ingredients (tomatoes, peppers, onions, carrots, and celery). Cook until tomatoes are soft, peppers blister, and onions are translucent. Add the chicken broth and water. Simmer until everything is very tender. Puree in blender, or with a hand mixer if available. Pass through strainer.

While you are pureeing the soup, begin heating the heavy cream—also in a large pot. Add the chicken base to the cream and whisk until incorporated. Add pureed soup to the cream and simmer. Reduce to thicken until desired consistency.

Season and serve. Enjoy!

YIELD

Serves 20

TAMAYO

When people think of gold in the Old West, they think of Sutter's Mill in California. Some even recall that gold was found in Colorado a decade later, but few are aware that the first gold found in Colorado was discovered in what is now the city of Denver.

In 1858, William Greenberry "Green" Russell and his party from Auraria, Georgia, discovered gold in the South Platte River near Cherry Creek. The news traveled fast, as of course miners and prospectors would arrive soon to seek their fortunes. But as in California, in Colorado the vast majority of arrivals came the following year, giving rise to the name *Fifty-Niners*.

A notable exception was William H. Larimer—who, along with a large party of men, ventured from Leavenworth in the early Kansas Territory to what is now Denver. Larimer helped form the Denver City Town Company, named after the then governor of the Kansas Territory.

The Fifty-Niners were unhappy with the great distance to the Kansas government and quickly sought separate territorial status. In 1859 they designated the area the Territory of Jefferson, which operated informally as an illegal entity until the bill for territorial status was passed by the U.S. Congress in 1861. William Gilpin was named the first territorial governor, and he chose the name *Colorado*. This is believed to be a rough translation of the Spanish word for colored.

As settlers arrived to search for wealth, the town began to grow into a major supply point. Soon, train routes were established to supplement the rough roads cutting through the mountains. Denver quickly became a regional hub for agriculture, meatpacking, and food processing. All frontier towns sprouted breweries, bakeries, hotels, and mercantile stores that sold equipment for farming and ranching, such as barbed wire, windmills, seed, feed, and harnesses.

The Mile High City (the official elevation is exactly 5,280 feet) is also home to numerous oil and gas firms. Tourism—fueled by winter sports such as skiing; summer sports such as fishing, horseback riding, hiking; and seasonal hunting—has helped to make Denver grow. The city is also home to a large contingent of federal employees, which includes those working for the U.S. Mint.

Tamayo is located in the original Hope Building. Built in 1888, with additions in 1893, it housed J. H. Howard's Jewelry shop in 1890 and the City Hall Pharmacy. From 1896 to the 1940s, it was the longtime home of the Hope Hotel. This same building also housed part of the renowned Laffite restaurant. A one-story addition on the corner of 14th and Larimer was made to the building in

1993. The addition once housed the Cadillac Ranch Steakhouse, and it is now home to Tamayo Restaurant and its remarkable rooftop patio.

Tamayo
1400 Larimer Street
Denver, Colorado 80202
(720) 946-1433

Calamari Azteca

Calamari in Adobo with Arugula and Plantain Puree

PLANTAIN PUREE

Preheat oven to 350 degrees. Place the plantains, in their skins, on a baking sheet. Roast for 45 minutes or until very soft to the touch. When cool enough to handle, peel off the skins and cut the plantains into chunks. In a small food processor or blender, blend together the plantains, cream, lemon juice, salt, and pepper until smooth. Keep warm.

CALAMARI

In a large skillet, heat the oil. Add the calamari and sauté for 2 minutes. Stir in the adobo sauce, lemon juice, honey, cilantro, salt, and pepper. Cook for another minute or so, until the calamari is tender—be careful not to overcook. Remove from heat. With tongs, remove the calamari from the skillet. When the calamari are cool enough to handle, stuff them with the arugula and then cut each body crosswise in half.

On each of four large dinner plates, spoon a portion of the plantain puree. Place the halved stuffed calamari on top, standing upright. Spoon the sauce from the skillet around the puree on each plate. Garnish the plate with chive oil if desired.

PLANTAIN PUREE

2 yellow-black plantains, soft to the touch

½ cup heavy cream

1 tablespoon freshly squeezed lemon juice

½ teaspoon salt

¼ teaspoon freshly ground black pepper

CALAMARI

2 teaspoons canola oil

12 ounces fresh calamari bodies, cleaned

½ cup adobo sauce

2 teaspoons freshly squeezed lemon juice

2 teaspoons of honey

¼ cup chopped fresh cilantro

¼ teaspoon salt

⅛ teaspoon freshly ground black pepper

1 bunch arugula, washed and dried, tough stems removed

chive oil (optional; recipe follows)

(continued on next page)

CHIVE OIL

1 cup canola oil

¼ cup chopped fresh chives

CHIVE OIL

In a blender, process together the oil and chives until smooth. This oil can be stored tightly covered for up to 1 week in the refrigerator. Bring to room temperature before using.

YIELD

Serves 4

Camarones al Chipotle

Tequila Flambé Shrimp

CHIPOTLE SAUCE WITH GOAT CHEESE

In a food processor or blender, combine all the sauce ingredients. Blend until sauce is a smooth puree. Adjust the seasoning with the honey. Using the back of a ladle or rubber spatula, force the sauce through a medium-mesh sieve placed over a bowl. This sauce can be stored for up to 3 days, tightly covered, in the refrigerator.

FRISÉE SALAD

In a medium bowl, toss together the frisée, lemon juice, salt, and pepper. Set aside.

SHRIMP

Preheat the oven to 350 degrees. In a large ovenproof skillet, heat the butter and oil over medium heat. Season the shrimp with the salt and pepper. Add the shrimp to the skillet. Carefully add the tequila. Tilt the skillet to ignite the tequila, and when the flames die out, stir in ¼ cup of the chipotle sauce.

Place the skillet in the oven and bake until the shrimp are curled and cooked through, about 2 minutes. Be careful not to overcook the shrimp, which is easy to do.

BLACK BEAN PUREE

In a large pot, heat the bacon and lard until the lard is melted and the bacon begins to render a little fat. Add

---

**CHIPOTLE SAUCE
WITH GOAT CHEESE**

½ cup crema fresca (or sour cream mixed with a little heavy cream)

½ cup chopped, seeded tomato

2 canned chipotle chilies in adobo sauce

1 tablespoon chopped fresh cilantro

2 tablespoons soft goat cheese

¼ cup chopped white Spanish onion

1–2 tablespoons honey, or to taste

¼ tablespoon salt

⅛ teaspoon freshly ground black pepper

FRISÉE SALAD

¼ pound frisée, trimmed and cleaned

2 teaspoons freshly squeezed lemon juice

¼ teaspoon salt

1 pinch freshly ground black pepper

SHRIMP

2 tablespoons butter

1 teaspoon canola oil

(continued on next page)

20 jumbo shrimp (11 to 15 per pound), peeled with tails intact and deveined

½ teaspoon salt

¼ teaspoon freshly ground black pepper

2 tablespoons tequila

BLACK BEAN PUREE

1 tablespoon chopped bacon

1 teaspoon lard or solid vegetable shortening

¼ cup chopped white Spanish onion

¼ cup epazote leaves

4 cups chicken stock or water

2 ounces dried black beans

salt and freshly ground black pepper to taste

TO SERVE

½ cup black bean puree

grated Cotija or Parmesan cheese to garnish

chive oil to garnish (optional)

the chopped onion and epazote leaves, if using, and sauté until the onion is softened, 10 to 15 minutes. Carefully add the stock. Cover and bring to a boil. Add the beans. Lower the heat and simmer, covered, until the beans are very tender, about 2 hours. The beans should be soupy—you should have about 13 cups liquid. Season with salt and pepper.

In a blender or food processor, puree the black beans, adding the black bean cooking liquid or chicken broth as needed for desired consistency. A good proportion is ⅓ cup of liquid to 1 cup of cooked beans. You can store the puree in the refrigerator for up to 3 days.

TO SERVE

In the center of each dinner plate, ladle a quarter of the chipotle sauce, warmed. Place 1 tablespoon of the black bean puree (recipe follows) in the center. Arrange 5 shrimps, standing up, spoke-fashion, on top of the black bean puree. Top with the frisée salad. Decorate the plate with drops of chive oil (optional) and sprinkle with Cotija cheese, if using.

YIELD

Serves 4

Chili en Nogada

Veal-Stuffed Poblano Chili with Walnut-Almond Sauce

NOGADA (WALNUT-ALMOND) SAUCE

Place walnuts and almonds in a blender. Pulse to finely grind. Add the cinnamon, nutmeg, and salt. Add ¼ cup of milk and blend to puree. Add the remaining milk and blend until smooth. Transfer to an airtight container and place in the refrigerator. The sauce is served chilled.

CHILIES AND STUFFING

Preheat the broiler. Place the whole chilies on the rack of a broiler pan. Broil about 4 inches from the heat, turning the chilies over occasionally, until they are evenly blackened on all sides, 15 to 20 minutes. Place the chilies in a paper or plastic bag and seal. Let stand until cool enough to handle and the skins have loosened, about 15 minutes. Remove skins. Cut a slit from the top of each chili down the side. Remove the seeds and veins. Set aside.

Next, prepare the stuffing. In a large skillet, heat the oil over medium heat. Add the onion and sauté until softened, about 5 minutes. For the last 2 minutes, add the garlic. Add the veal and salt and then sauté, breaking up the meat with a wooden spoon, about 8 minutes or until no longer pink. Add the tomatoes, raisins, almonds, and pine nuts. Cook over medium heat until

NOGADA (WALNUT-ALMOND) SAUCE

1¼ cups walnut pieces or halves

⅓ cup blanched sliced almonds

¼ teaspoon ground cinnamon

1 pinch of ground nutmeg

¼ teaspoon salt

1 cup of milk

CHILIES AND STUFFING

4 fresh large poblano chilies

1 tablespoon canola oil

1 white Spanish onion, chopped

2 cloves garlic, chopped

1 pound ground veal

¼ teaspoon salt

1 pound tomatoes, peeled, halved, seeded, and cut into ½-inch cubes

½ cup dark seedless raisins

⅓ cup blanched sliced almonds

3 tablespoons pine nuts

pomegranate seeds

cooked through and most of the liquid has evaporated, about 20 minutes. Spoon the stuffing into the chilies, dividing equally.

TO SERVE

In the center of each large salad plate, spoon a little nogada sauce. Place a stuffed chili in the center of each, and spoon more sauce over the chilies. Garnish with pomegranate seeds. Serve at room temperature.

❧ YIELD ❧
Serves 4

WYNKOOP BREWING COMPANY

The brewery's namesake, Edward Wanshaer (Ned) Wynkoop came to Denver in 1858, when the area was Arapahoe County, Kansas Territory. He had been born in Philadelphia in 1836. By 1858 he was living in Leavenworth, Kansas. His connections with the new governor of the western territory, James Denver, got him appointed sheriff for Arapahoe County, which would eventually become Colorado. By 1859, after joining the Larimer party while traveling west, he had arrived in Denver, the focus of most travel to the territory. Wynkoop (pronounced WINE-coop) is credited with suggesting that the community be named after the Kansas Territory governor, perhaps as a thank-you for being named sheriff.

Ned Wynkoop ran for city marshal in 1861 but lost the election. The Civil War gave him a new career. After being appointed captain in the 1st Colorado in 1862, Wynkoop participated in the Battle of Apache Canyon and earned a promotion to major. In 1864 Wynkoop became the post commander at Fort Lyon, and he was instrumental in convincing the Cheyenne Indians to forget their differences of the Indian Wars and to peaceably settle at Sand Creek under the protection of the U.S. Army. The Cheyenne agreed; but shortly after, Wynkoop was reassigned to Fort Riley in Kansas.

The new territorial governor of Colorado, John Evans, along with Colonel Chivington and his 3rd Colorado Volunteers, decided to put an end to the "Indian problem." The 3rd Colorado Volunteers attacked the Indian village at Sand Creek, killing more than 150 Indians, mostly women and children. Wynkoop is sometimes blamed for the massacre, but his actions suggest he not only meant well, but knew nothing of the planned attack. The governor and Colonel Chivington took advantage of the situation, but their efforts backfired—at least temporarily. The Cheyenne and Arapaho tribes waged war on white settlers for years after this incident.

The Wynkoop Brewing Company is Colorado's oldest brew pub. It was founded in 1988 in the historic J. S. Brown Mercantile Building. Built in 1899, the Mercantile Building was impressive for its time with hardwood floors, thick timber pillars, and pressed-tin ceilings. Miners, ranchers, and city folks furnished their frontier homes with goods from the Mercantile. The main floor, which is now the bar and restaurant, was the original showroom.

The second floor of the Mercantile is now Wynkoop Billiards, an elegant pool hall. There are 22 tables, two private pool rooms, and several dart lanes. The upstairs bar was rescued from the original tasting room of the old Tivoli Brewery across the street.

A Denver newspaper published these nice words about Ned Wynkoop in 1860: "Ned is considered by his personal friends a warm and genial companion, true as steel." The Wynkoop Brewing Company believes the same can be said of the pub that bears his name.

Wynkoop Brewing Company
1634 18th Street
Denver, Colorado 80202
(303) 297-2700

Gorgonzola-Ale Soup

In a large soup pot, bring the potatoes and onions to boil in the 2 quarts of water. Cook until the potatoes are soft, about 20–25 minutes.

Drain the potatoes and onions and reserve some of the potato water. Carefully puree the potatoes and onions in a food processor or blender, adding a little of the reserved water as necessary to help puree the potatoes. Return the pureed potatoes to the pot and add remaining ingredients. Bring to a simmer and adjust salt and pepper if necessary. Stir until cheese is melted.

You may thicken this soup with a little cornstarch slurry made with reserved cooking water if you like a thicker soup. Garnish with chopped green onions or chives and a dollop of sour cream if you like.

2 pounds red potatoes, peeled and coarsely chopped

1 medium yellow onion, coarsely chopped

2 quarts water

4 ounces Gorgonzola cheese

12 ounces Rail Yard Ale or another amber ale

2 cups chicken broth (if prepackaged, use low sodium)

1 cup heavy cream or half-and-half

2 teaspoons kosher salt

1 teaspoon ground white pepper

CRUST

½ cup granulated sugar

2 cups all-purpose flour

1 cup vegetable shortening

2 whole eggs

PEACH FILLING

3 pounds peaches, sliced frozen

3 tablespoons brandy

⅓ cup granulated sugar

BROWN SUGAR TOPPING

1 cup brown sugar

1½ cups all-purpose flour

¼ pound butter (salted is fine), softened

1 teaspoon ground cinnamon

¼ teaspoon ground nutmeg

2 tablespoons canola or other light oil

Peach Koopler

This original recipe, a perennial favorite at the restaurant, was devised by Mark Schiffler and Ron Robinson at some point shortly after the earth cooled. Peach koopler is great served with vanilla or cinnamon ice cream—or just a big blob of lightly sweetened whipped cream.

CRUST

Mix all ingredients well in the bowl of a stand mixer, food processor—or if you want to, grandma style in a big ceramic bowl with a strong wooden spoon. Mix until smooth and spread evenly in the bottom of an ungreased 9-by-13-inch casserole dish. Bake in 350-degree oven for about 30 minutes or until crust is lightly browned. Remove from oven and allow to cool for 15 to 20 minutes. Meanwhile . . .

PEACH FILLING

Mix all ingredients together and set aside until needed.

BROWN SUGAR TOPPING

Combine all ingredients and mix well together. A food processor is awesome for this project, but you can use an electric mixer or even your (God forbid!) clean hands.

When your crust has cooled, place the peach mixture on top and distribute evenly. Then put the brown sugar mixture on top and spread that evenly. Put in the 350-degree oven and bake for 1½ hours. Remove and allow to cool for about 30 minutes. Serve warm.

Note: You may make this recipe ahead and reheat in a 225-degree oven for 30 minutes (or reheat in the microwave). Oh, and this goes well with a Wynkoop Wixa Weiss with a lemon squeeze or even a glass of hearty Sagebrush Stout.

YIELD
Serves 8–10

PIE CRUST

¾ cup vegetable shortening
(or lard + 2 tablespoons
vegetable shortening)

2½ cups all-purpose flour, sifted

¼ teaspoon salt

⅓ cup ice-cold water

VEGETABLES

1½ cups diced carrots

1½ cups diced celery

1 tablespoon unsalted butter

1 teaspoon salt

½ teaspoon ground black pepper

1 teaspoon paprika (sweet is best)

LAMB MEAT AND SAUCE

¼ cup canola oil

2 pounds lamb stew meat

½ cup all-purpose flour

3 tablespoons minced shallots

1 tablespoon minced garlic

½ cup Burgundy or other
red wine

6 cups beef stock or bouillon

½ cup tomato paste

2 tablespoons minced
fresh rosemary

Shepherd's Pie

This dish has been served since the pub opened in October 1988. It may seem long and involved, but it is simple and can be spread out over a day or two. Use your favorite mashed potato recipe. For the pie crust you can use your favorite recipe, the recipe provided, or a pre-made crust from the grocery. If you make all the pie ingredients just before baking it, they will be warm and the baking time will be much shorter. The cooking times provided are based on cold ingredients.

PIE CRUST

In a medium-sized mixing bowl, cut the shortening into the flour with a pastry cutter or by using two butter knives. Add the salt and cold water, and mix the dough with your hands until mixture comes together. Do not overmix. Wrap dough in plastic and refrigerate for 30 minutes or until you are ready to use it.

VEGETABLES

In a large skillet or sauté pan, melt butter over medium heat. Add remaining ingredients and cook until vegetables just turn tender, about 10 minutes. They should still have some "bite" to them.

LAMB MEAT AND SAUCE

Heat oil in a large, heavy-bottomed Dutch oven or saucepan until hot. Season meat with salt and pepper.

Carefully add lamb meat to oil in pan, and brown meat on all sides. Do not crowd meat in pan! Cook in batches if necessary.

When meat is browned, add shallots and garlic and any set-aside lamb meat.

Sprinkle flour slowly over meat while stirring continually to avoid lumps. Once flour is incorporated, cook for 5 minutes, scraping the bottom of the pan to avoid burning.

Slowly add red wine and then stock, stirring continually. Add tomato paste, rosemary, and bay leaves and bring to a boil. Lower heat and simmer for 45 to 60 minutes or until meat is tender.

Strain meat from sauce and set meat aside to cool on a cookie sheet. Remove bay leaves. If cooking shepherd's pie immediately, cover the sauce and set it in a warm place. If you are going to cook the pie later, keep sauce uncovered in refrigerator until cool to the touch, then cover tightly. Either way, you will need to stir the sauce occasionally to keep a skin from forming.

TO ASSEMBLE THE PIE
Line a 9-by-13-inch glass or metal casserole dish with pastry dough, cutting away excess dough at top of dish. Spread 2 cups of the mashed potatoes evenly across the pie crust.

4 bay leaves

1 tablespoon salt

2 teaspoons black pepper, ground

TO ASSEMBLE THE PIE

4–6 cups mashed potatoes

1 recipe lamb sauce

1 recipe lamb meat

1 recipe pie crust

1 cup shredded Parmesan cheese

1 bunch green onions, chopped

Place half of the lamb meat on top of the potatoes. Top the lamb meat with all of the vegetable mixture and then add the remaining lamb meat. Cover this layer with enough mashed potatoes to fill casserole. Bake at 325 degrees for 1½ hours or until casserole reaches an internal temperature of 165 degrees.

Meanwhile, heat lamb sauce over low heat until hot. Remove pie from oven and top with Parmesan cheese; return pie to oven until cheese is lightly browned.

To serve the pie, ladle some sauce into a wide serving bowl and place a serving of pie on top. Garnish with some chopped green onions.

Front Range

ALPS BOULDER CANYON INN

The Alps Boulder Canyon Inn predates Colorado statehood by several years. Built before 1870 (Colorado became a state in 1876), the Alps was originally called the Topeka Colonies. Later owners named it the Hadley Cottages. The property was a stage stop and resting spot for the mass of humanity traveling to and from Boulder's mining districts.

In 1905 the property was completely remodeled and renamed the Alps Hotel and Resort. The Alps Resort provided a restaurant and luxurious accommodations for travelers on the Switzerland Trail Railroad. Built in 1883, the Switzerland Trail carried supplies and ore up Fourmile Canyon from Boulder to present-day Sunset. Wagons would complete the trip to Ward and Gold Hill.

In 1898, a passenger service opened and was dubbed the Switzerland Trail of America. The ads proclaimed, "One need not go to Switzerland for sublime mountain scenery." Trains carried 250 passengers and 100 tons of ore each day. The line traveled up Fourmile Canyon to Sunset, north to Gold Hill, and on to Ward. The line continued to the south and west from Ward.

Steep grades required powerful locomotive engines. In 1898 the Colorado & Northwestern (C&N) had three engines built that were the largest narrow-gauge locomotives in the world. Engine Number 30 is in Boulder's Central Park, at the corner of Broadway and Canyon.

Trains were sometimes loaded with kegs of beer packed in snow, and tourists rode the rails just for the experience. Every effort was made to make the line pay its way, but a decline in silver mining and a series of floods in lower Boulder Canyon proved to be too much. The old rails are gone; but portions of the Switzerland Trail can be driven by passenger car, bicycled, or hiked, and it still offers the same magnificent views that once made it famous.

The railway station was located 300 yards north of the Alps. Most guests back then arrived and departed by rail, but a few came by horseback or wagon. When rail travel declined, and finally ceased altogether, the Alps Hotel and Resort fell on hard times. The hotel was eventually closed and owners operated the property as a bordello, and then for a while it was "Art's Bar and Grill." The hotel's original liquor license was signed by Teddy Roosevelt.

After WWI, the property hosted one of Colorado's first trout farms. It was operated by the Boulder Fish and Game Club, the state's first conservation organization dedicated to stocking Colorado's high mountain lakes, rivers, and streams. The 1940s brought the Boulder Canyon Forest Highway, known today as Colorado Highway 119 or Boulder Canyon Drive, connecting Boulder and Nederland through scenic Boulder Canyon. The fish hatchery was relocated as the new highway passed in front of the Alps Hotel.

In 1960 the Alps became one of America's first Moose Lodges. The Moose Club operated for 30 years until it was sold in 1990 due to declining membership. After a two-year multimillion-dollar renovation, the Alps Hotel reopened as the Alps Boulder Canyon Inn. The Alps became Boulder's and one of Colorado's oldest lodging properties.

Alps Boulder Canyon Inn
38619 Boulder Canyon Drive
Boulder, Colorado 80302
(303) 444-5445

Alps Butter Pecan Belgian Waffles

2 eggs, separated

1½ cups whole milk

2 tablespoons baking powder

1 cup all-purpose flour

½ cup unsalted butter, melted

½ cup pecans, chopped (walnuts may be substituted)

This is a terrific waffle recipe, the best we have tasted. These waffles are easy to make and have a great buttery pecan flavor.

Preheat a waffle iron. Spray iron with nonstick spray before first waffle. In a bowl, whip the egg whites until stiff, but not dry. Set aside. In a separate bowl, food processor or blender, combine the egg yolks, milk, baking powder, flour, and melted butter. Beat until smooth. By hand, fold in the reserved egg whites and the chopped pecans. Proceed according to waffle iron manufacturer's directions. These waffles taste great with maple syrup or your favorite toppings. Garnish with pecan halves.

"All happiness depends on a leisurely breakfast."

—John Gunther

Alps Cowboy Cookies

Guests rave about these cookies, so there are always plenty on hand. Some are made with chocolate chips and some with raisins.

Preheat oven to 325 degrees. In a large bowl, cream together shortening and sugars. Add eggs and vanilla. In a separate bowl, sift together flour, baking soda, baking powder, and salt; add to the creamed mixture. In a separate bowl, combine oats, corn or bran flakes, and chocolate chips or raisins. Add to the dough mixture by hand. Bake at 325 degrees for 12 minutes or until the edges turn brown and the centers still look chewy.

1¼ cups butter-flavored Crisco

1 cup white granulated sugar

1 cup brown sugar

2 large eggs

1½ teaspoons vanilla extract

2½ cups all-purpose flour

1 teaspoon baking soda

½ teaspoon baking powder

½ teaspoon salt

1½ cups oats, rolled and dry

1¼ cups corn or bran flakes cereal

1 cup chocolate chips or raisins

CHAUTAUQUA DINING HALL

Chautauqua is an Iroquois word that means one of two things: either "two moccasins tied together" or "jumping fish." There is some vague similarity between those two translations, but the word also describes a lake in western New York known as Chautauqua Lake.

In 1874, John Heyl Vincent and Lewis Miller began a summer school for Sunday school teachers on the site of a Methodist camp. Eventually, it became known as the Chautauqua Institution. Their objective was to make teachers more professional. Their intent was educational, not religious, and the Institution was never affiliated with any specific denomination. Every faith was included, although Protestantism was the primary force leading the movement.

After only a few years, adult education of all kinds was the focus. They included correspondence courses designed to bring "a college outlook" to working and middle-class people. Along with the educational, arts, and public affairs offerings at Chautauqua, the many thousands of summer residents attended concerts and social activities. The Chautauqua Institution soon became known as a center for rather earnest, but high-minded, activities that aimed at intellectual and moral self-improvement as well as civic involvement. Theodore Roosevelt said that Chautauqua was "typically American, in that it is typical of America at its best."

Early in the 20th century, the "circuit chautauqua" became popular. The institutional chautauquas were not very fond of these traveling, tented chautauquas. Around 1915, at the height of the movement, 12,000 communities had hosted a chautauqua. The quality of the offerings varied from college-educated lecturers and Shakespeare plays to vaudeville and animal acts.

The movement had largely died out by the mid-1930s. Many observers credit the automobile and modern entertainment like radio, movies, and later television as the causes. Other considerations included religion. The increase in fundamentalism and evangelical Christianity in the 1920s conflicted with the nondenominationalism exhibited at most chautauquas. Many small, independent chautauquas were turned into church camps. And the Great Depression made chautauquas economically impossible for organizers and audiences.

July 4, 1898, was the opening day of the Colorado chautauqua. Several thousand people gathered together to create a cultural and educational summer retreat. Today, the Colorado chautauqua is one of only three remaining in the United States. And it is the only site west of the Mississippi River, in continuous operation, with its original structures intact.

Located at the base of Boulder's Flatirons, Chautauqua Park is on the National Register of Historic Places and is a local landmark. The Colorado Chautauqua facility offers the Auditorium (built in 1898), voted one of the top 10 places artists love to play because of its superior acoustics; the Dining Hall (1898), open all year; the Academic Hall (1900), housing administrative offices; and the Community House (1918), an excellent example of Arts and Crafts architecture.

Boulder's facility is the only year-round chautauqua, and the only one whose grounds are open to the public—with free admission. It is a place where couples, families, and friends can delight in a nature hike in the hills, concerts or festivals in the park, and gourmet food on a beautiful porch. The Chautauqua Dining Hall's reputation as a must-visit restaurant has developed over the last decade. Enjoy classic American cuisine featuring natural and local products.

Chautauqua Dining Hall
900 Baseline
Boulder, Colorado 80302
(303) 442-3282
(303) 440-3776

6 cups mayonnaise

1 cup dill relish

2½ ounces lemon juice

1 teaspoon black pepper

1½ teaspoons kosher salt

3 tablespoons Dijon mustard

3 tablespoons fresh parsley, chopped

½ yellow onion

3 carrots

1 large onion

⅛ pound butter

1 can (#10) of canned plum tomatoes

⅛ gallon whole milk

salt to taste

Tartar Sauce

Combine all ingredients, mixing well. Store in refrigerator.

Cream of Tomato Soup

Sweat carrots and onion in butter. Add remaining ingredients and simmer for 30 to 45 minutes.

Puree until very fine consistency and pass through a strainer if necessary. Season with salt to taste.

Guacamole

Peel the avocados. Combine the avocado meat with all the other ingredients and stir together. Chill and serve.

"There are those who seek in other climes
the joys they might have known.
Mid the mountains and the meadows of
the land they call their own.
I would find shady canyons,
where at night the gentle dew
comes to kiss the rose and heliotrope—
when stars are all in view.
I would stand amid these mountains,
with their hueless caps of snow.
Looking down the distant valley,
stretching far away below:
And with reverential rapture
thank my maker for this grand
peerless, priceless panorama,
that a child can understand."

—Cy Warman, "poet laureate of the Rockies,"
described the Gunnison country in
sentimental terms in 1900.

12 avocados

1½ medium red onions,
   diced small

2–3 jalapenos, diced small

12 medium Roma tomatoes,
   diced

5 teaspoons salt

6 tablespoons lemon juice

2 tablespoons finely chopped
   fresh cilantro

COLORADO CATTLE COMPANY

The history of the Colorado Cattle Company, as told by a ranch hand:

Well, not countin' the pre-historic man and the Injuns, the history of this ranch began in the mid 1800s. In them days, a man named John Iliff ran cattle all over this country. He ran cattle from up near the Colorado Mountains to Kansas and from Wyoming to the South Platte River. In 1868 he set up a base camp nearby and changed the direction of the cattle drives heading north. They came there for fresh horses and decent food. Yep, the Goodnight/Loving trail traveled right over this here country.

Mr. Iliff set up a line camp shack just a few miles from where our homestead is located today and his cowboys took care of thousands of head of cattle out here on the plains. When the government in Washington D.C. decided to populate this here country, they started the Homestead Act. A family could get up to 320 acres of free land just by tilling up a part of it, planting it to crops and building a house on it. After a few years, the government would just give it to you for being there. Sounded pretty good to farmers starved out for space back East and many came out here and tried to make it go.

This didn't sit too well with our Mr. Iliff. He started fencing the public lands with that new barbed wire so only his cattle could graze there. He was a sharp one! Not only did he fence in public land to graze, he had his cowboys homestead on 160 acres around every water source he could find and then he bought it from them. When President Cleveland realized what all was going on out here, he passed a law that made the cattle barons remove all fencing from public lands and that was the beginning of the end of the great days of the Iliff Cattle Company.

The winter of 1886–87 was really, really tough. Thousands of head of cattle froze or starved to death, the cattle market in Chicago fell through, and many of the huge ranchers went broke—including John Iliff. By then this here ranch was being homesteaded as part of the land rush and homesteaders were starting to plow it up and try to make a go of it. One of them was named Leonard Biggs. He homesteaded on this ranch and built a house out of sod and rock in the early1880s that is still standing and in use today! We use it for a mechanical and utility room. A few years back we had a plumbing break inside and I'll be durned if the sod didn't grow as soon as it got wet!

Leonard went up to Kimball, Nebraska, in 1897 and bought a load of logs off the train there to start building onto the soddie. By then many of the homesteaders had folded up and traded their land off to him for whatever they needed to get out of Colorado and move back East. His ranch was growing quickly and he had good water so he became more and more successful. The stagecoach route came through the ranch briefly since he had horses to trade, food, water, and a place to stay for their customers.

In the meantime, he kept adding on to the ranch as people droughted out or gave up and left. He built two log additions on to his sod house, which we call the bunkhouse and now use for our guests. By the time he sold out, he owned almost 20,000 acres including what is now Colorado Cattle Company—named in honor of the old Cattle Companies that were originally located in this area of Colorado.

They fixed up the bunkhouse and started right into the guest business in the summer of 1992. Since then, they have been trying to share the cowboy ways with their guests and teach them a bit about the Old West. Their mission is to teach the guests the ways of doing things in the West, teach them to rope and work a cow, and generally turn them from greenhorns to cowboys. Our ranch cooks turn out some purty good grub too—here are a few recipes from our camp kitchen.

Colorado Cattle Company
70008 WCR 132
New Raymer, Colorado 80742
(970) 437-5345

COWBOY LINGO

brand: burned ownership mark on cattle. "This is my brand."

burning daylight: wasting time. "We're burning daylight."

cowboy gear: to trot. "Hit cowboy gear."

dude: not local, from somewhere else. "He's a dude."

goner: lost, dying or dead. "That cow is a goner."

Head 'em up and move 'em out: gather the cows together and start them moving. "Let's head 'em up and move 'em out."

herd: a group of cows, horses or people. "Gather the herd."

84

Howdy, pardner: Hello, friend.

jingling: gathering horses. "Go jingle in the horses."

outfit: ranch or pickup truck. "Nice outfit."

plum played out: absolutely exhausted. "That horse is plum played out."

skedaddle: run like hell. "Let's skedaddle!"

greenhorn: new to the ranching business. "He's a greenhorn."

CC and Cattle Kate's Ribs

Note: Ingredients are per pound of ribs.

Mix barbecue sauce, onion, mustard, and brown sugar and simmer on low fire until onion is tender. Set aside.

Brown ribs in skillet and dust with garlic powder. Place ribs in pot of boiling water and cook for 20 minutes. Drain and rinse.

Boil the ribs again in beer for another 20 minutes. Add water to cover if needed. Drain and rinse.

Cover ribs with sauce mixture, and let them marinate until ready to cook. Cook on fire or grill until heated through; or you can cook them in the oven on a foil-lined pan at 350 degrees for about 15–25 minutes, until ribs look dry and are starting to crisp on the edges.

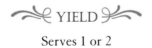

YIELD

Serves 1 or 2

1 pound pork ribs, country style

garlic powder

2 tablespoons mustard

3 tablespoons brown sugar

1 onion, finely diced

½ jar barbecue sauce

12 ounces beer
(we use Budweiser)

6 small boneless chicken breasts, or leftover chicken

8 tablespoons butter

1 cup cream of mushroom soup

1 cup grated cheddar cheese

8 ounces elbow macaroni, cooked

1 tablespoon finely diced onion

4 tablespoons flour

1 cup chicken stock or bullion

1 cup diced celery

1 green pepper, diced

1 small jar pimentos, drained and rinsed (added for color—you can use red bell peppers too)

CCC Chuckwagon Chicken

Dice leftover chicken or boneless breasts and toss with flour. Using butter, lightly brown chicken breasts in a skillet over low heat until no longer pink. Mix all other ingredients into butter-chicken mixture and put in greased baking dish. Cook at 350 degrees for 30–45 minutes until cheese is melted and mixture is bubbling. Top should just start to brown.

⤜ YIELD ⤛
Serves 6

CCC Appaloosa Cake

Mix eggs, vanilla, sugar, and oil. Add flour, salt, soda, and cinnamon and beat well until pretty smooth. Add apples and nuts and stir. Pour into greased and floured Bundt pan and bake for 1 hour and 15 minutes at 350 degrees. Turn the pan over and remove the cake. Sometimes you need to loosen it with a spatula or butter knife.

Serve with ice cream or vanilla sauce.

3 eggs

1 teaspoon salt

3 cups diced apples

2 teaspoons vanilla

1½ teaspoons baking soda

1 cup chopped nuts (optional)

2 cups sugar

½ teaspoon cinnamon

1 cup oil

3 cups flour

2 cups self-rising flour

12 ounces beer (Budweiser
   is our favorite)

4 tablespoons sugar

4 tablespoons butter

CCC Cowboy Beer Bread

Mix flour and sugar, pour in a can of beer, and mix. Place into greased loaf pan and bake at 350 degrees for 20 minutes. Melt butter and pour carefully over the bread in loaf pan and continue baking an additional 20 minutes or until bread is crusty and golden brown. Run knife around edges of pan to release and remove from pan. Let cool a bit before cutting, or it will fall apart. To make a sweet dough for shortcake, increase the sugar to 8 tablespoons and follow the same recipe.

✤ YIELD ✤
Makes 1 loaf

"You can rub out cow trails with highways, swap sage-brush for cities, and free range grass for filling stations, but you can't cure the West of bein' 'howdy country.'"

—A Colorado cowboy

COOPERSMITH'S PUB & BREWERY

The great Colorado gold rush of 1858–59 was not responsible for the development of this community—although the flood of emigrants headed west because of gold, silver, and free land was. The fertile fields of the Colorado Piedmont and the abundant river water attracted a great number of homesteaders in the early 1860s. The Cache la Poudre (pronounced *POO-der*) River was named for a powder cache left by French fur traders during a bitter winter.

Indians were a problem for the homesteaders, mainly because they were well established in the area, having lived here for hundreds of years. They hardly recognized the right of the United States to govern the land as a result of the Louisiana Purchase in 1803. The Arapaho continued to live in villages near the mountains, coexisting peacefully with the settlers despite the loss of their hunting grounds on the eastern plains by treaty in 1861.

The Sioux became hostile to white encroachment further north, forcing the relocation of the Emigrant Trail from the North Platte River to the South Platte valley. The Pawnee and other tribes on the Colorado eastern plains also initiated hostile incidents. Concerned for the safety of the settlers, Colonel William O. Collins—commandant of Fort Laramie, the regional headquarters of the U.S. Army—ordered that an outpost be built.

The initial camp, commissioned on July 22, 1862, and named for Colonel Collins, was constructed and manned by the 9th Kansas Volunteer Cavalry. The mission of the fort was to protect the emigrant trains and Overland Stage lines on the Overland Trail from the growing hostile attacks of the Plains Indians. The camp was founded near the settlement of Laporte (originally called Colona) that had been founded in 1858 by homesteaders.

During its first two years, the fort saw little direct action, so stockade-type walls were never built. Several changes of military units eventually brought Company F of the 11th Ohio Cavalry. They arrived just in time for the flooding on the Poudre River in June 1864. The camp was substantially destroyed, and a better site was needed. A local homesteader volunteered a new site adjacent to his own claim four miles downstream on the Poudre, on a section of high ground. Colonel Collins issued orders relocating the camp, by then known as Fort Collins.

The new site also saw little direct action, but its proximity to the growing community of homesteaders made it the center of local commerce. The subsiding of the conflict with the Indian tribes, and their complete removal from the Colorado Territory after 1865, made the fort unnecessary. In September 1866 the post was completely abandoned by order of General William T. Sherman.

As farmers settled in the outlying areas, other settlers began moving to the new town, where they opened stores, livery stables, and other businesses. The first buildings of the state agricultural college (present-day Colorado State University, situated in Fort Collins by vote of the state legislature) were erected in the 1870s.

In 1873, the city of Fort Collins was founded. The area prospered, first as a center for quarrying and farming and by 1910 for sugar-beet processing. Emigrants such as Henry and Katherine Bauer of Lincoln, Nebraska (the author's grandparents), who fled their German community along the Volga River in Russia at the turn of the century to come to the Midwest, worked the sugar-beet fields every season. Beets made sugar, but the tops proved to be excellent and abundant food for local sheep. By the early 1900s the area was being referred to as "Lamb feeding capital of the world."

The site of Fort Collins itself is in present-day Old Town, between Jefferson Avenue (the old Denver Road) and the Poudre River. The 300-foot-square parade ground, standard for forts of its type, was centered at the present intersection of Willow and Linden Streets.

Fort Collins was a conservative city in the 20th century, with prohibition of alcoholic beverages from the late 1890s until 1969. Today, there is a thriving beer culture. The city has three microbreweries and several brewpubs, including CooperSmith's Pub & Brewery, a local mainstay since 1989. The annual Colorado Brewer's Festival is held during late June in the Old Town area.

A redbrick pedestrian walkway, flanked by street lamps and surrounding a bubbling fountain, is the focus of this restored historic district, which offers a look at the earliest roots of the city. Come for lunch, dinner, a midnight snack, or just to wet your whistle. The food is great, but if beer is not your pleasure, CooperSmith's carries one of the largest single malt scotch selections in all of northern Colorado.

CooperSmith's Pub & Brewery
5 Old Town Square
Fort Collins, Colorado 80524
(970) 498-0483

Cheese and Artichoke Dip

Drain and dice artichoke hearts. Chop the scallion using both white and green parts. Add all ingredients except Parmesan to a large mixing bowl. Mix well. Keep cold until ready to serve.

Microwave a serving portion until warm. This may also be done on a stove. Place warmed portion in ovenproof serving dish. Top with grated Parmesan cheese and broil until the dip begins to bubble or top begins to brown. Place serving dish on large platter with an assortment of fresh vegetables and crackers for dipping. A fresh bread bowl makes a nice—and edible—serving dish.

YIELD
Makes 3 cups

1 cup artichoke hearts

2 scallions, chopped

1 cup mayonnaise

½ cup sour cream

1 tablespoon dry white wine

½ teaspoon white pepper

1 cup grated Parmesan cheese

1 tablespoon butter

½ yellow onion, finely diced

½ bunch celery, washed and diced

½ cup diced tomatoes

3 ounces tomato paste

1 tablespoon honey

½ pound mushrooms, sliced

1½ quarts water

⅛ pound vegetable stock base

1 teaspoon sea salt

1 teaspoon black pepper

1 teaspoon garlic powder

½ teaspoon onion powder

1 teaspoon oregano

1 teaspoon basil

⅛ cup chopped parsley

1½ cups Parmesan, shredded

½ cup heavy table cream

Tomato and Mushroom Bisque

Melt butter in a large stockpot. Sauté the onion and celery until tender, about 5 minutes. Add the rest of the ingredients, except the Parmesan and cream, to the vegetables. Simmer for 30 minutes. Turn off the heat.

Add the Parmesan and cream while whisking the soup vigorously. Simmer for 10 minutes. Serve warm with beer bread.

YIELD
Makes ½ gallon

"Black pepper heat and comfort the brain."

—John Gerard's *Herball*, 1597

Highland Cottage Pie

LAMB AND SAUCE

Preheat oven to 450 degrees. Place lamb, bay leaves, and rosemary in a large roasting pan. In a large mixing bowl, combine salt, Horsetooth Stout, beef broth, tomato paste, garlic, black pepper, and red wine. Whisk until thoroughly combined. Pour the stout mixture over the lamb. Put roasting pan in oven and cook lamb mixture for 20 minutes or until lamb is cooked through. Remove pan from oven.

Using a slotted spoon, remove lamb from the stock, putting back any bay leaves or rosemary that is taken out with the meat. Refrigerate the lamb until well chilled. Tightly cover until ready to use.

Meanwhile, transfer the stock to a large saucepan and keep hot, just below a simmer. Add the butter to a heavy 4-quart saucepan set over low heat. Melt the butter, stir in flour, and form a paste. Allow the flour-butter mixture (roux) to cook over low heat for 5–6 minutes, stirring occasionally. The roux will become blond in color and have the aroma of toasted almonds.

Increase heat to medium, add 2 cups of the hot stock to the roux, and whisk until the mixture is smooth and begins to bubble. Follow with the remaining stock in three additions, each time whisking until the sauce is smooth and has returned to a simmer.

LAMB AND SAUCE

2½ pounds trimmed lamb brochette meat, in ½-inch pieces

1 tablespoon fresh rosemary, whole leaves

3 bay leaves

2 teaspoons salt

¼ cup Horsetooth Stout

2 quarts low-sodium beef broth

¼ cup tomato paste

1½ teaspoons minced garlic

1½ teaspoons black pepper

¼ cup dry red wine

¼ pound butter

1 cup all-purpose flour

FILLING

2 large carrots, peeled and cut into ¼-inch dice

1 stalk celery, ¼-inch dice

½ teaspoon paprika

1 tablespoon butter

4 pounds (3 quarts) mashed potatoes, chilled

12 ounces pie dough, chilled

GARNISH

1¼ cups grated Parmesan cheese

Allow the sauce to simmer for 10 minutes. Remove from heat and strain, discarding the bay leaves and rosemary. Pour sauce into a large baking dish and refrigerate until completely chilled. Cover until ready to use. The sauce and lamb may be made the day ahead. Reheat sauce to a simmer before serving.

FILLING

Place a sauté pan over medium heat. Add 1 tablespoon butter. When the butter has melted and started to foam, add the carrots, celery, and paprika. Sauté until vegetables are tender but still crisp, 4–5 minutes. Transfer vegetables to a plate and refrigerate until completely chilled. Vegetables may be prepared one day ahead.

TO ASSEMBLE

Assemble the cottage pie in a 13-by-9-inch baking pan. Preheat oven to 375 degrees. Roll the pie dough out to a 15-by-11-inch rectangle. Place the pie dough in the baking pan so that ½ to 1 inch of the dough overhangs the pan on all sides. Spread half of the chilled mashed potatoes over bottom of the crust. Spread the chilled vegetables and lamb evenly over the mashed potatoes. Top vegetable-lamb layer with remaining mashed potatoes. Form overhanging dough into a decorative edge. Loosely cover cottage pie with baking paper and aluminum foil.

Place cottage pie in oven and bake 45 minutes. Remove baking paper and aluminum foil and bake for an additional 15 minutes until the top and crust have nicely browned. The cottage pie should reach an internal temperature of 170 degrees.

GARNISH

Remove cottage pie from the oven and let rest for 10 minutes. Cut cottage pie into nine rectangular pieces. Spread ½ cup of the sauce on a serving plate and top with a piece of cottage pie; garnish with more sauce and 2 tablespoons of Parmesan. Repeat with the remaining pieces of cottage pie. Serve immediately.

YIELD

Serves 9

HOTEL BOULDERADO

The nomadic Southern Arapaho Indian tribe frequently wintered in the Boulder area at the base of the foothills. Ute, Cheyenne, Comanche, and Sioux Indians also passed through the area, and Native Americans dominated the landscape until gold was discovered in Colorado. When the tens of thousands of "Fifty-Niners" arrived to search for the precious metal in 1859, this part of Colorado was included in the Nebraska Territory. The actual boundary of the Kansas and Nebraska Territories is the Baseline Road in Boulder.

While gold was not as plentiful as most hoped, the discovery of silver brought another wave of humanity to the territory. Boulder grew slowly as it supported prospectors, miners, businessmen, and gamblers in their quest for fortune. Boulder City was incorporated in 1871, and in 1873, the railroad was extended to serve the community. Statehood was achieved in 1876, and the Union Pacific Railroad built the Boulder Railroad Depot in 1890.

In 1905, Boulder was a city of 8,000 and growing very slowly. The city council thought it ought to be growing faster than it was. As they evaluated their situation, they decided that one of the drawbacks to a higher growth rate was the lack of the "comfort of a first-class hotel." They sold stock at $100 a share to raise the construction funds. The Commercial Association said, "We have invested our money in the enterprise because it represents Boulder's greatest need. We shall be glad of returns, but shall be infinitely gladder if we secure a hotel of such beauty of proportions and architectural design that it will stand as a monument to her pride in her enterprises. Let it be the Hotel Beautiful."

They ultimately named it after "Boulder" and "Colorado" so that no guest would forget where he had been. The Hotel Boulderado has been a downtown Boulder landmark since it opened on New Year's Day, 1909. To provide guests with modern comforts, all rooms were fitted with light fixtures that ran on both natural gas and electricity. Men were busy 24 hours a day in the basement, stoking the huge coal furnace to provide hot water and keep the hotel properly heated. Telephones were installed in most of the 75 rooms. Room prices varied from $1.00 to $2.50 per day.

Designed by William Redding & Son, the hotel is a combination of Italian Renaissance style with Spanish Revival features. The four corner towers; the pairs of tall, narrow windows; and the bracketed cornices are indicative of the Italianate style. The iron railings on the large side porches, arched fourth-floor windows, and curvilinear gables are all Spanish Revival features.

When entering the hotel from either Spruce or 13th Street, the hotel's original foundation is clearly visible—large blocks of orange-red sandstone from the former Colorado Red Sandstone

Company of Fort Collins. The thousands of red bricks in the original historic building are believed to have come from the old Thompson Pressed Brickworks, located on land that is now part of the University of Colorado Campus. The bricks were intricately laid in rows four deep for warmth and durability.

Inside the hotel's main entrance and to the left is the Emporium Gift Shop. Early in the hotel's history, this was the ladies' writing room and parlor. Another famous feature is the original cantilevered cherrywood staircase, extending from the basement to the fifth floor. The balcony overlooking the lobby is a popular photography point. Many couples have exchanged their wedding vows here throughout the years.

The entire mosaic tile floor in the entryway, lobby, and dining room is original, as is the Otis elevator in the lobby. A hotel employee has to manually operate the elevator cab, which serves the guest floors. The original safe is still behind the front desk, and some of the hotel's archived guest registers are on display by the 13th Street entrance. The water fountain to the left of the front desk dates to the days when the Arapaho Glacier supplied most of Boulder's water.

In the hotel lobby's south entryway are large glass cases displaying historical artifacts from the hotel and Boulder. Throughout the lobby and along the skywalk to the North Wing, you'll find framed newspaper articles, old menus, and historic photographs of the hotel and the Boulder area.

Famous hotel guests have included Helen Keller, Douglas Fairbanks, Ethel Barrymore, and Louis Armstrong. The city council of 1905 could never have envisioned what the Hotel Boulderado would become—or that the city would someday be the site of the nation's atomic clock.

Hotel Boulderado
2115 13th Street
Boulder, Colorado 80302
(303) 442-4344

¼ cup sesame oil

5 cups canola oil

1½ cups rice wine vinegar

5 pasteurized egg yolks

1 tablespoon Dijon mustard

1½ tablespoons onion powder

1½ tablespoons garlic powder

½ cup pineapple juice

2 tablespoons lemon juice

2 tablespoons lime juice

zest from 1 lemon and lime,
    finely chopped

¼ cup honey

salt and pepper to taste

Citrus Vinaigrette

Combine egg yolks, onion and garlic powder, and mustard in blender or food processor. Turn on machine and alternately add oils and vinegar until you have used two-thirds of it.

While machine is still running, add honey and juices; then add the rest of the oils and vinegar. Turn off machine and stir in zest; season with salt and pepper to taste. Vinaigrette should be emulsified. Serve over your favorite salad.

YIELD
Makes 2 quarts

Grilled Atlantic Salmon
with Caramelized Red Onion Marmalade

SALMON

Grill on presentation side (flesh side) for 2 minutes. Turn on skin side for 1 minute. Remove from grill and place fish in preheated 350-degree oven for 4 to 5 minutes. Serve topped with room-temperature red onion marmalade.

CARAMELIZED RED ONION MARMALADE
Makes 2 cups

Sauté onions in olive oil until they begin to caramelize. Reduce heat and add brown sugar, vinegars, and red wine. Cook over low heat until all liquid is absorbed into onions and you have a thick and chunky consistency.

Stir in the melted butter and raspberry preserves. Cook until the preserves are thoroughly incorporated.

YIELD
Serves 6

SALMON

six 6- to 7-ounce portions Atlantic salmon with skin removed, rubbed with extra virgin olive oil, coarse sea salt, and fresh cracked pepper

CARAMELIZED RED ONION MARMALADE

1 red onion, julienned

½ yellow onion, julienned

¼ cup brown sugar

⅛ cup apple cider vinegar

1 tablespoon red wine vinegar

1 tablespoon red wine

1 tablespoon extra virgin olive oil

1 tablespoon butter, melted

1 tablespoon raspberry preserves

salt and pepper to taste

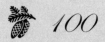

1 pound butter, cubed

3 cups sugar

8 eggs

2 teaspoons vanilla extract

2 teaspoons Grand Marnier

8 cups flour

3 teaspoons baking powder

½ teaspoon salt

3 cups coarsely chopped
pistachios

1 cup chocolate, melted

Chocolate-Dipped Biscotti

In mixer, cream together butter and sugar. Combine eggs, vanilla extract, and Grand Marnier. Mix into the creamed butter and sugar. Add all dry ingredients and pistachios and mix just until dough forms.

Form into four equal-sized logs about ¾ inch thick. Bake at 350 degrees for 15 minutes; rotate and bake another 15 minutes until logs are golden brown.

Allow logs to cool for about 1 hour.

Then cut the logs crosswise about ½ inch thick and toast in the oven for 4 to 5 minutes. Allow the cookies to cool for 15 minutes, and then dip half the cookie (lengthwise) in melted chocolate. Place cookies on waxed paper and leave until chocolate is set and they are ready to serve.

YIELD
Makes about 7 dozen cookies

THE PECK HOUSE

The great rush for gold and silver in the last half of the 19th century created the town of Empire. Prospectors from New York named it after the state, believing that someday it would be just as great as their home state. Hundreds of gold and silver mines attracted tens of thousands of people, all hoping to get rich. James Peck and his three teenage sons arrived in 1860 to build a house so other family members might follow. In 1862, Mary Grace Parsons Peck arrived with the family's possessions by oxcart. As another wave of prospectors arrived from the East to invest in their mines, Mrs. Peck became a full-time innkeeper and cook.

Empire and The Peck House were established just before the Civil War reached the area. The battle at Glorieta Pass in New Mexico was fought by Union troops from Colorado, and the regiment was filled largely with young men from Empire. After hundreds of casualties on both sides, the Union troops won; the Confederates retreated to Santa Fe. This battle essentially ended the plan to extend the Confederate lines across the southern part of the territory to southern sympathizers in California.

Mining in the area accelerated after the war ended. In 1875, huge deposits of silver were discovered in Leadville. With Empire surrounded by mountains, many of the miners headed for the silver strike elected to look in the immediate area. The Peck House added more rooms and a new dining area. To accommodate the boarders and townspeople, the Lake Michigan ship's bell over the hotel door was rung three times a day to call the men around town to dinner as well as to announce the arrival of the daily coach coming through from Central City to Georgetown.

James Peck was killed in 1880 when he fell from his carriage on Union Pass. Mrs. Peck and her oldest son, Frank, took over the family business of running The Peck House as well as the mines. The Peck House became the social center of Clear Creek County when another addition was built. A billiard room, bar, and poker room were added downstairs along with several new guest rooms upstairs. A new law ordered all bars to have a library for the education of the miners, resulting in the addition of a ladies' parlor and library.

The original hotel guest register shows that Generals Greenville M. Dodge, William Tecumseh Sherman, and Ulysses S. Grant stayed at the Peck House. Also, Phineas T. Barnum was a guest when he visited the area as part of the temperance movement.

The hotel remained in the Peck family until the death of James Peck's grandson, Howard, in 1945. Owners since then have included Margaret Collbran and Louise Harrison (granddaughters of Adolph Coors, the founder of Coors Brewing Company) and Henry Collbran, one of the founders

of the Midland Railroad. The survival of The Peck House is at least partly due to basic structural restoration done between 1950 and 1968 by the two women. At one point they renamed the place the Hotel Splendide and modeled it after a small European hotel.

In 1980 the present owners, Gary and Sally St. Clair, visited The Peck House while on their honeymoon. They fell in love with it and by March 1981 had arranged to buy it. Just like the Pecks had done more than 120 years earlier, they brought their three teenage children with them to share in the dream. Today you will often find Sally at the front of the house or in the extensive gardens, while Gary is slaving away in the kitchen to produce the unusual and creative cuisine for which the hotel has won awards.

The Peck House
83 Sunny Avenue
PO Box 428
Empire, Colorado 80438
(303) 569-9870

Salmon Vera Cruz

Roast, peel, seed, and dice the peppers. Roast, peel, and coarsely chop the garlic. Combine all sauce ingredients in a saucepan, heat thoroughly, and serve over the cooked salmon filets.

Chopped jalapeno, habanero, or other hot peppers may also be added if you like your food really hot. This sauce is also great on grilled steak, chicken, or any other seafood.

⊱ YIELD ⊰
Serves 4

"A meal without salt is no meal."

—Hebrew Proverb

four 6-ounce boneless, skinless salmon filets (use any desired method to cook salmon)

1 red bell pepper

1 yellow bell pepper

1 Anaheim chili pepper

2 tablespoons chopped fresh cilantro

8 cloves garlic

½ cup olive oil

2 tablespoons sugar

salt and pepper to taste

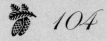
¼ cup mushrooms, sliced

3 tablespoons golden raisins

2 heaping tablespoons Major
    Grey's Chutney

¼ teaspoon curry powder

dash cayenne pepper

dash Worcestershire sauce

½ cup heavy cream

20 large shrimp, shelled
    and deveined

3 cups long grain and wild rice,
    cooked

Shrimp Sarah

Cook mushrooms, raisins, chutney, spices, Worcestershire sauce, and cream in a small skillet over medium heat for 5 minutes, or until thickened. Arrange the shrimp on four skewers.

Brush the shrimp with a little melted butter, oil, or margarine. Broil 4 to 5 inches from the heat for 4 to 5 minutes, turning once or until cooked. Serve on rice with sauce.

YIELD

Serves 4

THE STANLEY HOTEL

The Stanley Hotel has been named as one of America's most haunted hotels. Its ghostly stories are told by guests and staff alike. Stephen King's *The Shining* had The Stanley Hotel as its infamous inspiration.

Actually, it was due to very poor health that the famous F. O. Stanley moved west. In 1903 he arrived in Estes Park, Colorado, and soon endeavored to change the area's local economy into a more dynamic and vibrant one. Lord Dunraven sold Mr. Stanley 160 acres of real estate.

F. O. Stanley built the road from Lyons so his visitors could travel in a Stanley Steamer to the sprawling, gleaming Stanley Hotel. The historically significant, steam-driven vehicle was a means to transport visitors to a resort area by automobile rather than the usual mode of transportation by train—for the first time in American history.

Twins Freelan O. and Francis E. Stanley began their car company after selling their dry photographic business to Eastman Kodak. The history of the Stanley Steamer began when it was produced by the Stanley Motor Carriage Company. The company was in business from 1902 through 1917. The Stanley Rocket actually set the world land speed record at 127.7 miles per hour on the Daytona Beach Road Course in 1906, driven by Fred Marriott. Unbelievably, it still holds the land speed record for a steam car. In 1917 over 500 cars were produced. Stanley Steamers were later overtaken by the internal combustion engine as technology marched on, and the last Steamer was produced in 1927.

In 1907, groundbreaking for The Stanley Hotel's main building was begun. Timber cut from Rocky Mountain National Park provided strong and sturdy support beams. The Bear Lake burn in 1900 provided a way to furnish the timber for the huge undertaking of constructing such an enormous hotel. The faint smell of smoke is said to still linger in the wood.

F. O. Stanley passed away in 1940, leaving behind not only the magnificent red-roofed hotel but also a power and water company as well as a sewer company. Its centennial year has given the Stanley Hotel a revered place in Colorado history. The magnificent house beckons delighted visitors each year. Stanley built the main portion of the famous hotel and eventually completed 10 more buildings of the complex, which graces Estes Park against a majestic backdrop of purple mountain ranges.

Today 55 acres make up the beautiful surroundings, and most of the original buildings are currently utilized. Wildlife abounds on the grounds, and a Stanley Steamer is proudly displayed in the lovely lobby. The Cascades Restaurant is a luxurious setting for fine dining, including continental and regional dishes as well as an extensive wine list. The Cascades Bar is a relaxing way to enjoy bar food and dinner. The Steamer Café serves some great gourmet coffee and elegant pastries.

The Stanley Hotel
333 Wonderview Avenue
Estes Park, Colorado 80517
(800) 976-1377
(970) 586-3371

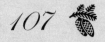

The Stanley Salad

CANDIED PECANS

Mix egg whites, cayenne, confectionary sugar, and salt. Whip until medium-soft peaks form.

Gently fold in pecans. Place on baking sheet and bake until golden brown. Hold at room temperature until ready to serve.

BLACKBERRY VINAIGRETTE

In a blender, mix all ingredients except oil. Blend thoroughly until you have an even texture. Then add the oil in a thin stream while blender is still running. Once oil has been incorporated, transfer the vinaigrette to a container and hold in refrigerator until ready for use.

ELK MEDALLIONS

Season meat and cook in a skillet, but preferably on the grill, until desired internal temperature is reached. Hold for about 5 minutes to rest the meat and allow the juices to flow back.

TO ASSEMBLE SALAD

Mix spring lettuce with vinaigrette, candied pecans, sunflower sprouts, mint leaves, and sliced figs. Place ingredients in the middle of plate or platter. Slice tenderloin into thin slices and arrange as imagination inspires.

YIELD
Serves 4

---

spring lettuce

candied pecans (recipe follows)

blackberry vinaigrette
(recipe follows)

sunflower sprouts

mint leaves

6 fresh figs, sliced

elk medallions (recipe follows)

CANDIED PECANS

½ pound pecan halves

3 egg whites

1 teaspoon cayenne pepper

1 teaspoon confectionary sugar

1 pinch salt

BLACKBERRY VINAIGRETTE

1 pint fresh blackberries

1 cup sherry vinegar

1 tablespoon Dijon mustard

1½ cups canola oil

1 teaspoon pure honey

ELK MEDALLIONS

four 6-ounce elk tenderloins

⅛ cup chopped fresh thyme

salt to taste

pepper to taste

SYLVAN DALE GUEST RANCH

"The sense of well-being and comfort experienced at Sylvan Dale is supported by its history." One thousand years ago, people found shelter in the shallow cave in Echo Rock. The Indian tribes wintered in the valley, seeking refuge from the snows of the high country. In the 1800s people sought healing from respiratory ailments in the clear, clean mountain air.

In the beginning, in the early 1920s, Mr. and Mrs. Frend Neville owned a small cattle ranch at the mouth of the Big Thompson River. Wealthy doctors from St. Louis came to the area to hunt deer and liked it so much they wanted to bring their families. The Nevilles then built some cabins and a lodge along the river, planted some apple trees, and named it *Sylvan Dale*, meaning "wooded valley."

Years later, the facilities were sold to Cotner College, a Christian church school in Lincoln, Nebraska. But during the Depression of the 1930s, Cotner College closed and Sylvan Dale was leased out as a youth camp. Maurice Jessup, then a college kid in Oklahoma, overheard a conversation about the ranch and asked for a summer job there. He hitchhiked to Loveland and caught a ride from town with the mail carrier. He was overwhelmed by the beauty of the mountains and the rushing water and immediately told the camp director Mr. Weldon, "You know, I just love this place. Someday I'm going to own Sylvan Dale."

That was in 1934. Twelve years later, the ranch was for sale and Maurice Jessup was in the military. He received special permission to go and bid on the property. After scratching his bid on a piece of paper, Maurice and his wife Mayme ("Tillie") were awarded the 125-acre, rundown property. Over 61 years later, the ranch is still in the Jessup family and continues to enchant people from near and far.

Through a lifetime of hopes and dreams solidly based on faith, dedication, and hard work, the Jessups and their two children, David and Susan, increased the 125-acre ranch to a 3,200-acre working guest ranch. The Big Thompson flood of 1976 threatened to put an end to the dream, but reconstruction efforts were successful; and what was once a summer guest ranch became a year-round facility that has blessed folks for over 50 years.

The future of Sylvan Dale remains with the Jessup Family, and so do the rich traditions of its past. It all adds up to a deep-rooted sense of belonging. You can taste it in the hot buttered biscuits—light as a feather. You can hear it in the distant cry of the coyote, the soft sound of the wind in the

pines, and mostly in the warm Western welcome that still rings true: "Pull up a chair, join our family table. Rest . . . Relax . . . Enjoy." This is what life is all about . . . Sylvan Dale Guest Ranch.

A TRIBUTE

We will never forget the afternoon of May 12, 1993. The Sylvan Dale valley was incredibly beautiful, clad in a spring robe of lush green sprinkled with the magic of wildflowers. We gathered on the lawn of the "J" House, facing to the west. The hills of home embraced us as we sat close sharing the memories of our dad—Maurice Jessup, a man who lived his values, patiently endured his long illness, unselfishly gave opportunity to troubled youth, and shared his dream with literally thousands of people. We said goodbye to him that afternoon as his ashes drifted into the valley. Our dad lived in the present moment. He was a "doer," a risk-taker, a dreamer . . . a man with incredible vision and faith. His legacy continues to enrich our lives.

—Susan Jessup

Sylvan Dale Guest Ranch
2939 N. County Road 31D
Loveland, Colorado 80538
(866) 611-6972

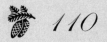

2 eggs, slightly beaten

1 package active dry yeast

½ cup sugar

1 cup raisins

1½ teaspoons salt

6 cups flour

¼ cup margarine, soft

1 egg beaten with 1 tablespoon
    milk (for glaze)

2½ cups milk

Hefenkranz
a German bread

"Three or four of the Loechner daughters worked at the ranch in the early days. Mrs. Loechner would come to visit once a week and I'd hear them all talking and laughing. She would always bring a loaf of Hefenkranz with her. Her daughter Eleanor got the recipe for me from watching her mom make it—since she never measured anything."

—Tillie

Proof the yeast in ¼ cup warm water. Plump the raisins in boiling water for 10 minutes; then drain and set aside. Scald milk until hot enough to melt butter, and stir in the sugar. When milk cools to lukewarm, add the proofed yeast, then the slightly beaten eggs, salt, and enough flour to make a firm dough. Knead until smooth and satiny. Let rise until doubled in size. Punch down, add the raisins, and let rise again.

Put dough on a floured board and divide into two equal parts. Then divide each part into three pieces. Roll each of the three parts into rolls about 16 inches long for braiding. Braid and shape into loaves, pinching the ends firmly so the loaf will keep its shape. Let rise until doubled. Brush the tops with egg glaze before baking at 325 degrees for about 40 minutes.

Carrot Cookies

Mix first four ingredients in a bowl. Add mashed carrots and orange zest. Sift dry ingredients together (flour, baking powder, and salt). Add to wet mixture and stir until mixed. Drop dough by teaspoonfuls onto a greased cookie sheet. Bake 15 minutes at 350 degrees until slightly browned. Cool cookies and top with powdered sugar icing.

 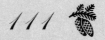

2 eggs, beaten

⅔ cup oil

⅔ cup sugar

¼ teaspoon vanilla

1½ cups flour

1½ teaspoons baking powder

½ teaspoon salt

2 teaspoons orange zest

⅔ cup mashed carrots

1 cup milk

2½ cups flour

1 tablespoon white vinegar

2 teaspoon baking soda

2 sticks margarine

½ teaspoon salt

2 cups sugar

1 cup hot water

2 eggs

1 teaspoon vanilla

½ cup cocoa

Mahogany Cake

Mix together milk and white vinegar and set aside. In a separate bowl, cream together margarine, sugar, eggs, and cocoa. Add milk mixture. Then add flour, baking soda, and salt. Add hot water and vanilla, and mix thoroughly. Bake for 45 minutes at 350 degrees (in greased 8-by-11-inch pan) until a toothpick or broom straw comes out clean.

TWIN OWLS
STEAKHOUSE

It is generally accepted knowledge that American Indians were the first inhabitants of Colorado. That is true relative to our modern recorded history; but archaeological evidence shows that the Clovis people, who crossed the Bering Strait when a glacial land bridge existed, lived in this area thousands of years ago. Other Paleo-Indian cultures used the contours of the Estes Valley to channel game into the hands of waiting hunters.

The crystal-clear lakes full of fish, mountain meadows that supported all manner of game, and relatively mild seasonal weather attracted the Ute Indians to Estes Valley, where they often summered. Unwelcome visitors included the Arapaho tribes looking for game and the Mexican explorers looking for gold. Both of these groups succeeded in removing the Utes from the area; but they too were replaced by the white man, who came in search of first fur trapping and trading and then gold and silver.

Joel Estes was an adventurer from Kentucky who had gotten rich in California in 1849. Only 10 years later, he "discovered" the valley now named for him. With little gold to be found in the area, he decided to bring his wife and 13 children here to settle down. During the 6 years the Estes family lived here, the owner and editor of the *Rocky Mountain News* visited them, and he named the valley after his host.

Estes left in 1866 after selling to Griff Evans, who established a dude ranch on the Estes homestead. Cattle ranches also flourished in the 1870s. The McGregor Ranch is still in operation. The Elkhorn Lodge was built to accommodate the larger number of tourists who came to the valley. One particular guest was Francis Stanley. He had developed a valuable photographic process and was credited with co-inventing the Stanley Steamer with his twin brother, Freelan.

Francis was having health problems, and he discovered that the cool, clear mountain air was quite beneficial to his health. He moved permanently to the valley and built the Stanley Hotel in 1909. Stephen King wrote much of *The Shining* while staying at the Stanley Hotel.

The Twin Owls Steakhouse was originally built as a home for the Wayne Stacey family in 1929. It was bought in 1965 by Dr. Curry Meyers, who converted it into the Meyers 3M Guest Ranch. The house was turned into a restaurant and later named the Black Canyon Inn for its views of Black Canyon. The Steakhouse uses only organically grown, grass-fed beef. The cattle are fed only a cow's

natural diet, so patrons are eating the healthiest beef available. The restaurant dress code is "Colorado casual."

Estes Park is 7,522 feet above sea level in a mountain valley. Surrounded by snowcapped peaks ranging from 8,500 to more than 14,000 feet high, it is readily accessible by car. Estes Park's reputation as a resort destination has attracted such notables as Pope John Paul II, the Emperor of Japan, and President George W. Bush.

Twin Owls Steakhouse
Located at the Black Canyon Inn
800 MacGregor Avenue
Estes Park, Colorado 80517
(970) 586-9344

Spanish Flan

Melt 2 cups of sugar over low heat until it becomes a brown syrup. Pour a small amount in bottoms of soup cups and turn cup around to coat walls. (Do only two cups at a time because sugar hardens fast.) Let the cups sit for 20 minutes.

Beat eggs, cream, and sugar. Add sugar and vanilla and beat. Fill cups to top. Place cups in pan with sides so you can add water to pan. Keep water level near top of cups. Bake for 45 minutes to 1 hour at 350 degrees or until firm.

Turn off oven and let the cups sit for 30 minutes more in oven.

Refrigerate for at least 3 hours. To serve, run a knife around edges of each cup, put a dessert plate on top of the cup, and quickly flip it over.

YIELD
Serves 12

2 cups pasteurized egg yolks

½ cup pasteurized egg whites (or 24 large eggs, beaten to froth)

7 cups heavy cream

1 cup half-and-half

6 cups sugar

3 tablespoons vanilla

Split Pea and Ham Soup

2 pounds dried split peas

2 red onions, diced

1 bunch celery, diced

3 carrots, diced

3–4 gallons water

3 ounces ham base
     or bullion cubes

1 pound ham, diced

black pepper

granulated garlic

2 tablespoons diced fresh garlic

4 tablespoons dried thyme

¾ cup olive oil

Put oil and seasonings in large pot and simmer for 5 minutes. Add ham and simmer 5 minutes more. Add peas and 2 gallons of water. Bring to boil for 10 minutes.

Add all vegetables. Add ham base and bring to boil. Add remaining water and bring to boil. Let it sit in the refrigerator overnight.

Reheat to serve. Add water if needed.

Mushroom Ragout

This ragout is served under a pine-nut-crusted chicken breast.

Put all seasonings and oil in pot; simmer for 3 minutes. Add pancetta and simmer 5 minutes. Add porcini mushrooms and dried mushrooms and boil 10 minutes. Add button mushrooms, chicken base, and water; boil for 10 minutes.

Thicken mixture with cornstarch mixed with cold water. Simmer on low heat for 10 minutes, adding water and wine as needed.

"I hate people who are not serious about their meals."

—Oscar Wilde

1 pound porcini mushrooms, cut in half

2 pounds dried mushrooms (forest blend)

3 pounds fresh button mushrooms, chopped

1 cup chopped pancetta

3 ounces chicken base

¾ cup olive oil

2 tablespoons chopped garlic

2 tablespoons granulated garlic

2 tablespoons black pepper

3 tablespoons dried thyme

1 quart red wine

1 quart water

cornstarch

Roasted Red Pepper-Coconut Sauce

4 ounces coconut milk

4 ounces roasted red peppers, diced small

1 quart heavy cream

¼ cup honey

2 tablespoons sea salt

2 teaspoons powdered ginger

1 tablespoon chopped fresh garlic

1 tablespoon white pepper

1 tablespoon cayenne pepper

1 cup sherry wine

⅓ cup olive oil

2 tablespoons of dried dill weed

cornstarch

This sauce is served with pasta and couscous.

Add all spices and oil to bottom of pot. Simmer until garlic starts to toast. Add sherry, coconut milk, and heavy cream and bring to boil; then reduce heat. Add cornstarch that has been mixed with cold water to thicken. Simmer 5 minutes, and then add roasted red peppers and honey. Simmer some more.

Great with penne pasta and chicken or couscous.

Northwest

ANDERSON RANCH

Native Americans first visited the Snowmass area during the summers. The Ute Indians hunted and fished here among the abundant mountains and valleys. Their preference for lower climates during the winter months was evidenced by their reference to the mountain as "Cold Woman," because it was often shrouded with clouds that they were certain was the reason for the occasional bad weather.

The first American explorers arrived in 1853 as part of the Gunnison survey. Led by Captain John Williams Gunnison of the Topographical Engineers, the survey was commissioned by the Secretary of War to find a railroad route to the West. Gunnison had achieved some national fame by visiting the Mormon communities and publishing the first detailed account of their lifestyle and religious practices in 1852.

As a man already experienced with exploration of the West, Gunnison was out to prove that an alternative existed to a route previously explored by John Fremont in 1848. After passing through the area and recording their findings, Gunnison and part of his party were later massacred by Paiute Indians along the Sevier River in Utah. Their early efforts would lead to more detailed surveys and more settlers.

By the 1880s the local Indians had been pushed out of this valley, and numerous ranches were established. Sheep and cattle occupied much of the ranchers' efforts, and a community developed. The local mountain was still subject to occasional bouts of bad weather in the winter months, and the settlers began to refer to it as "Snow Mass," reflecting the great abundance of snow that fell.

Charles Hoagland, an immigrant from Sweden, was a prominent rancher of the day. He had been hired to close the famous Smuggler Silver Mine in Aspen after the silver crash of 1893, and moved his family to the Brush Creek Valley to farm and ranch. Several of the buildings he erected, including the main house where they lived, are now part of the Anderson Ranch Arts Center.

Hoagland's daughter, Hildur, was raised on this ranch. She lived there for 40 years, attending the local one-room schoolhouse known at the time as the Brush Creek Frontier School (today called The Little Red Schoolhouse). Today, after more than 110 years in existence, the schoolhouse serves as an early childhood learning center. Hildur actually served as a teacher at this school. When she married Bill Anderson, the name stuck to the ranch as she inherited it and raised four children here.

Life at Anderson Ranch continued for decades until 1958, when Olympic skier Bill Janss discovered the area while visiting nearby Aspen. After deciding he wanted to build a world-class European-style ski community here, Janss began buying up ranches and soon controlled over 3,000 acres. In 1967 Snowmass-At-Aspen opened with multiple hotels, restaurants, and chairlifts and 50 miles of ski trails. The town was incorporated in 1977.

Anderson Ranch was transformed into an artists' community in 1973 after a group of artists from Aspen and the Roaring Fork Valley had cleared out the historic barns for studios. They set up a gallery and inaugurated an informal workshop program. Since its incorporation as a nonprofit visual arts community, Anderson Ranch has matured into a widely recognized institution that "promotes the imagination of young people, revitalizes the expressive impulse of adults, encourages the inventive experimentation of talented emerging artists, and supports the intensive inquiry and production of mature artists."

Anderson Ranch
PO Box 5598
5263 Owl Creek Road
Snowmass Village, Colorado 81615
(970) 923-3181

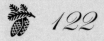

⅔ cup sugar

⅔ cup packed light brown sugar

1 cup softened butter

2 large eggs

½ teaspoon almond extract
  (not imitation)

1 teaspoon baking soda

½ teaspoon baking powder

½ teaspoon salt

1 cup all-purpose flour

3 cups old-fashioned oatmeal

½ cup almonds, sliced

1 cup golden raisins

1 cup butterscotch chips

Casebeer Cookies

Anderson Ranch is home to artists year-round, and its campus cafeteria creates art of a culinary style. Chef Lynn Knutson is known for providing a different homemade cookie every day for lunch, and she estimates the cafeteria serves 10,000 to 15,000 cookies each summer. Casebeer cookies are a favorite of Doug Casebeer, the director of Ceramics and Sculpture.

Preheat oven to 350 degrees. Cream butter with both sugars until smooth (in an electric mixer or by hand). Add eggs and almond extract.

In a separate bowl, mix flour, baking soda, baking powder, and salt. Add to butter mixture and mix well. Stir in oats, almonds, raisins, and butterscotch chips. Using an ice cream scoop, drop dough onto a cookie sheet, preferably covered with parchment. Flatten a bit with the heel of your hand.

Bake 8–10 minutes or until golden brown.

YIELD
Makes 2 dozen cookies

Spicy Thai Tomato Soup (Vegan)

We always get requests for this recipe . . . people can't believe how simple it is. Try it on a cold day with a gourmet grilled cheese sandwich!

In a large saucepan over medium heat, combine vegetarian stock, tomatoes, ginger, and chili sauce until hot. Remove from heat. Puree in a blender until smooth and return to saucepan. Add coconut milk and cook until hot. Garnish with cilantro or green onions.

1½ cups good-quality vegetarian soup stock

one 28-ounce can diced tomatoes

2 tablespoons minced fresh ginger or 2 teaspoons powdered ginger

½–¾ cup sweet Thai chili sauce (Mae Ploy brand is best)

½ cup coconut milk (light coconut milk also works well)

chopped cilantro or green onions for garnish

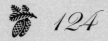

2 cups quinoa

3 cups mushroom stock

½ cup toasted pine nuts

1 cup fresh assorted wild mushrooms

1 cup fresh haricots verts (baby green beans), blanched

½ cup chopped fresh flat-leaf parsley

3 tablespoons white truffle oil (or plain olive oil)

salt and freshly ground pepper to taste

chopped fresh chives for garnish

Quinoa Salad
with Wild Mushrooms, Pine Nuts, and Haricots Verts (Vegan)

We created this dish for our annual art auction, which is our major fund-raiser. . . . This year's theme was "Colorado," so we wanted foods that were earthy and healthy. We used as much local produce and Colorado-made products as possible. We got great feedback on this dish.

Cook the quinoa in mushroom stock. (It gives the dish more flavor and some essential salt.) Sauté mushrooms in a little olive oil and chopped garlic until soft.

In a large bowl, combine quinoa, pine nuts, mushrooms, green beans, and parsley. Drizzle with white truffle oil. Season with salt and pepper, and garnish with fresh chives.

Parshall's Bar Lazy J Guest Ranch offers an excellent opportunity to experience some of the state's rustic history. Photo by Steve Bauer.

Denver's Castle Marne is a luxurious urban bed and breakfast. Photo by Steve Bauer.

The Devil's Thumb Ranch in Tabernash is a unique and environmentally sensitive resort. Photo by Steve Bauer.

Hotel Boulderado has been a downtown Boulder landmark since it opened in 1909. Photo by Beverly Silva.

Boulderado Lobby. Photo by Paul Dizon.

The Chilled Maine Lobster Salad is one of the delectable specialties at Denver's Hotel Teatro. Courtesy of Hotel Teatro.

Hot Springs Lodge & Pool in Glenwood Springs is a blend of the past and present. Photo by Kjell Mitchell, Hot Springs Lodge & Pool.

Anderson Ranch is located in scenic Snowmass Village. Courtesy of Snowmass Village; photo by Biege Jones.

Sylvan Dale Guest Ranch in Loveland is a historic working horse and cattle ranch. Photo by Steve Bauer.

The Stanley Hotel overlooks Estes Park, the gateway to the Rockies. Photo by Steve Bauer.

Tamayo is located in a historic 1888 Denver building and features a fabulous rooftop terrace. Photo by Linda Bauer.

The Historic Oxford Hotel is located in the heart of Denver's bustling downtown. Compliments of McCormick's Catering at The Oxford Hotel.

ATMOSPHERE BISTRO

Nestled in the mountains of northwest Colorado is the small town of Glenwood Springs. Nestled in this small town is the Atmosphere Bistro restaurant. Also nestled in Glenwood Springs is the grave of one of the Wild West's most colorful characters.

The Ute Indians settled in this area hundreds of years ago. Drawn by the plentiful wild game and fishing, the Native Americans found this location ideal. When the white man came to search for gold, he also discovered silver, lead, and of all things, healing waters. Captain Richard Sopris came to the area in 1860 and found many hot springs that were later commercialized as therapeutic treatments.

In 1879, Fort Defiance was built near Glenwood Springs. This was a log fort erected by prospectors who were trespassing on the Ute Reservation. Located 10 miles southeast of the prospectors' campsite at Carbonate, the fort gave its name to the town growing out of the camp. In 1883, Sarah Cooper, wife of founding father Isaac Cooper, had the town renamed Glenwood Springs, after her hometown of Glenwood, Iowa. She didn't like the name Defiance. Glenwood Springs was incorporated in August 1885.

Its location at the confluence of the Colorado River and the Roaring Fork River, as well gaining a stop on the railroad, historically made Glenwood Springs a center of commerce in the area. The city has seen some famous visitors—including President Teddy Roosevelt, who spent an entire summer vacation living out of the historic Hotel Colorado.

The Wild West legend, Doc Holliday, spent the final months of his life in Glenwood Springs. John Henry "Doc" Holliday was born in Griffin, Georgia, in 1851. Doc Holliday really was a doctor. He graduated from the Pennsylvania College of Dental Surgery in Philadelphia and practiced dentistry in several states. Besides dentistry, he was a gambler—dealing faro and consorting with everyone associated with saloons. Some of his arguments resulted in the death of another individual, giving him legend status long before he died.

It was in Tombstone, Arizona, that he was immortalized. There, Doc Holliday, the Earp brothers, and the cattle-rustling Clantons were involved in the famous shoot-out at the OK Corral on October 26, 1881. Years later, Doc Holliday, suffering from advanced tuberculosis, came to Glenwood Springs, hoping that the hot springs would help him. He died there and was buried in Linwood Cemetery, although the exact location of his grave is not known.

A visit to Glenwood Springs and Atmosphere Bistro offers travelers a unique historical experience as well as fine dining.

Atmosphere Bistro
817½ Grand Avenue
Glenwood Springs, Colorado 81601
(970) 945-6644

Rhubarb Marmalade, Cantaloupe, and Mango Salad

Peel the fruits and take out the seeds. Pit and cut into small cubes. In a large bowl, mix the fruit with the sugar and the vinegar. Reserve for 1 hour in the refrigerator.

Peel the rhubarb and cut into 1½-inch pieces. Add the rhubarb pieces to a pan with the brown sugar, lemon juice, and 1 tablespoon of water. Cook slowly over medium-low heat.

When the rhubarb is cooked (takes about 20 minutes), add the chopped tarragon leaves. Refrigerate for 30 minutes.

Spoon some of the rhubarb marmalade in the middle of a dish. Place the mango and cantaloupe salad around the rhubarb. Scoop some vanilla ice cream and place it on top.

4 rhubarb stalks

2 tablespoons crystal sugar

20 leaves fresh tarragon, chopped

½ ounce lemon juice

1 medium cantaloupe

1 mango

1 teaspoon balsamic vinegar

3 tablespoons brown sugar

vanilla ice cream

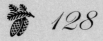

6 rabbit legs

13 ounces whole-grain mustard

1 bay leaf

1 teaspoon fresh thyme

½ cup canola oil

¼ cup white wine

1 carrot

1 onion

juice of 1 lemon

1 cup heavy cream

salt and pepper

Leg of Rabbit "à la Moutarde"

Peel the carrot and onion and dice very small. Preheat oven to 325 degrees. Season rabbit legs with salt and pepper. Sear rabbit, and add bay leaf and thyme. Mix together the mustard, lemon juice, and white wine. Add mixture to the rabbit.

Place the rabbit in a baking dish and cover. Bake for 45 minutes. When the rabbit is cooked, pour the liquids off into a saucepan. Add heavy cream and reduce over medium heat. Season sauce with salt and pepper. Place the rabbit into a serving dish and cover with the mustard sauce.

Sea Scallops "au Vert"

SCALLOPS

Peel the carrot and the onion. Wash scallops with cold water. Preheat a fry pan and add olive oil. When the oil is close to smoking, add the scallops. Sear on both sides. Season with salt and pepper.

In a saucepan, add the onion and carrot. Begin to sauté in olive oil. Dice the fish and place into the pan. Add white wine and cover with water. Cook 30 minutes and drain excess liquid.

FRENCH DRESSING

Place mustard, salt, and red wine vinegar into a blender. On medium speed, slowly add olive oil. When thick, add finely minced chives and pepper. Continue blending until the dressing is green.

TO SERVE

Put two scallops on the shell with fish mixture and dress with the French dressing. Garnish with fresh chives.

YIELD
Serves 3

SCALLOPS

6 whole sea scallops with shells

13 ounces halibut or other white fish

1 onion, finely diced

1 carrot, finely diced

1 cup white wine

2 tablespoons olive oil

FRENCH DRESSING

1 tablespoon mustard

1 tablespoon red wine vinegar

1 bunch of chives

salt and black pepper to taste

BAR LAZY J
GUEST RANCH

The early days of Colorado's development are all about white men coming to search for beaver pelts and then for gold, silver, lead, and coal. It did not take them long to discover what the Native Americans had known for centuries—Colorado's rolling hills and mountain fields were well suited for the buffalo and wild game that thrived in the area.

Miners and prospectors often brought their families with them, and industrious wives and children set up housekeeping. Frequently this was done in one of the camps that later turned into towns; but occasionally, they employed the agricultural skills they brought with them and started ranches. When the gold and silver deposits gave out, the agricultural pursuits became much more important to Colorado's survival.

Travelers through the area often approached farms and ranches looking for a meal and possibly a place to sleep. In the early days, most ranchers would not turn away visitors, particularly in inclement weather. Food and lodging were usually shared with complete strangers.

As time passed and the traffic along the more traveled routes increased, helping strangers became a real chore. Many ranches began to charge for food and lodging, even though they did not advertise for guests. Eventually, some ranchers went out of their way to offer these services. Some ranches operated like hotels, and when the travelers turned into tourists, they became known as "dude ranches," or a ranch that took in guests who were more at home in towns and cities, and not accustomed to ranch life.

Miss Lizzie Sullivan owned what was then known as the Buckhorn Lodge until 1904. She had been the superintendent of Grand County since 1896 but was ready to give up ranch life. James Ferguson and Edgar Messiter bought the ranch from Lizzie Sullivan and turned it into a resort in 1912. When James died, Edgar married his widow, Florence (Brownie). They decided to promote the ranch commercially and hired a young debutante who acted as their social secretary. Guests needed a letter of reference before they could hope to come to Buckhorn. And the elite of Colorado came. Back then the rate was $5/day for the American plan. This included food, lodging, horseback riding, fishing, square dancing, singing, and all cookouts.

Early guests stayed in tents along the river. Gradually, individual cabins were built for each family. Nearby, a smaller cabin housed the maids and governesses. At first everything was formal—coffee served in demitasse cups on the lawn, polo playing, and a croquet court between the cabins and river. Maids served their particular families and then returned to their quarters. Brownie supervised the help, and Edgar did all the outside work.

The Messiters sold the ranch in 1945, and it passed through a succession of owners. In 1952, Rudy and Mabel Menghini bought the ranch and changed the name to Bar Lazy J, which was the original brand for the ranch when it was first opened. Other owners added modern conveniences along the way, including renovating the cabins and putting in a heated swimming pool. A new barn houses the horses that carry guests on scenic trail rides.

The original Buckhorn Lodge, continuing in operation as the Bar Lazy J Guest Ranch, is believed to be the oldest continuously operating guest ranch in Colorado. Located along the scenic Colorado River, this dude ranch offers an excellent opportunity to experience some of the state's rustic history.

Bar Lazy J Guest Ranch
PO Box N
447 County Road 3
Parshall, Colorado 80468
(800) 396-6279
(970) 725-3437

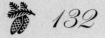

1 cup chili powder

½ cup ground cumin

¼ cup minced garlic

1 cup paprika

1 cup kosher salt

2 tablespoons ground
black pepper

½ cup brown sugar

Navajo Rub for Roast Pork or Prime Rib

This rub can also be used to accent fajita meat or Tex-Mex stew meat.

Combine all ingredients and rub on pork or prime rib, being careful not to contaminate any extra rub that you plan to store for future use. Cook the meat in your desired manner. Any leftover rub can stored in the pantry.

"Givers of great dinners know few enemies."

—Martial, ca. AD 95

Mushroom Dip

Flame-grill the artichoke hearts to give them "grill marks." Set them aside to cool.

Carefully cream the creamed cheese. Thoroughly mix all the remaining ingredients except the onions, and fold all spices into the cheese.

Fry the mushroom pieces in corn oil, and when they are soft, add the minced onion. Remove from heat when the onion is translucent and cool.

Fold the mushrooms and onions carefully into the cheese mix, and place the combined mixture in soufflé cups. Serve warm with shredded Romano cheese and crudités or vegetable bagel chips.

YIELD
Serves 20

3 large portobello mushrooms, diced

1 tablespoon corn oil

1 medium onion, minced and reserved

1 pound cream cheese at room temperature

1 teaspoon cumin

1 teaspoon garlic

1 tablespoon basil

½ teaspoon cayenne pepper

1 teaspoon kosher salt

½ teaspoon black pepper

2 teaspoons Worcestershire sauce

½ lemon, juiced and zest minced

3 artichoke hearts, diced

5 ounces goat or feta cheese

FILLING

6 red delicious or Granny Smith apples, peeled and sliced

1½ cups sugar

⅓ cup cornstarch

3 tablespoons cinnamon

1 teaspoon allspice

1 teaspoon nutmeg

TOPPING

2 teaspoons butter

½ pound melted butter

2 cups rolled oats

2 cups flour

½ cup white sugar

2½ cups brown sugar

Apple Crisp

Mix the dry filling ingredients together extra well. Toss in apple pieces and shake well for 1 minute. Place in an 8-by-8-inch or 10-by-10-inch pan. Then mix the topping ingredients, being careful to mix the brown sugar in last. Cover the filling with topping and bake at 350 degrees for 1 hour or until the internal temperature reaches 165 degrees.

YIELD
Serves 10

C LAZY U RANCH

Ranching was a natural outgrowth of the rush into Colorado for first furs, then gold and silver. The state's majestic beauty as well as the health benefits derived from the clean mountain air also brought many tourists seeking to enjoy the great outdoors. City dwellers seemed to thrive on the idea of visiting a working ranch and perhaps helping with the chores, always intending to return to the comforts of their metropolitan homes. Dude ranches sprang up across the state to accommodate these part-time cowhands.

The story of the C Lazy U began before 1919, when Jack Smillie was running cattle through the area and stayed at the Dexter Ranch, just across the road. The Dexter House is currently used for staff residence, but from 1900 to 1910 it was a post office and stagecoach stop. Jack returned to the Dexter Ranch in 1919 to marry Gertrude, one of the Dexter daughters. To house his new family, he bought the F Slash Ranch next door—now the C Lazy U—from Mr. Dow. The property was originally in the Curtis family that gave the name to the Curtis Ridge north of the lodge.

Jack Smillie built the barn without side wings in 1925. He also built several other structures that are still standing: the Meadow House, River House, old Bunk House, Spring House, Aspen House, and Bird's Nest. The Ranch House was home for the Smillies with a kitchen and dining room for their guests. Today that house has wings A through D and a lower-level office.

The small log structure between the Ranch House and the Lodge was the bathhouse, which contained his-and-her showers. At the time, a bathhouse was considered a luxury for a dude ranch. Jack also built the root cellar. This small log building housed the Delco Dynamo generator that supplied electricity for the ranch. The root cellar is next to Mare's Nest behind the Lodge.

Operating as a dude ranch, the owners could lodge two dozen guests and offered horseback riding, trout fishing, and bear hunting—plus all the great food and freshly baked pies prepared by Gertrude Smillie. Guests paid $40 a week or $125 a month during the 1930s.

After 20 years, the Smillies sold the ranch, and it passed through a succession of owners. In 1946, Dick and Katie Schoenberger bought out a partner and renamed the F Slash Ranch. At the time, Willow Creek's meandering course, when viewed from above, appeared to spell out a C with a U on its side underneath it—so they named it the C Lazy U Ranch.

Dick and Katie Schoenberger brought a dose of New York sophistication to complement the ranch's rustic charm. The ranch began a new era of success. Today we call it rustic elegance. Construction on the Lodge began in 1947. Lodgepole pine logs were felled on the Baldy hillside and dragged to the site by Jeeps. Skilled carpenters stripped, notched, and joined the logs with such craftsmanship that their expert work is still admired today by guests. The Lodge has been the focus of the ranch for dining and entertaining ever since.

In 1948 the east and west wings were built, adding and connecting six guest rooms to the Lodge. The ranch was then suitable for year-round entertaining of guests, and family-oriented activities brought both parents and children out to enjoy a dude ranch vacation.

Dick Schoenberger died in 1963, and Katie operated the ranch until 1973. Its present-day owners, the Murray family of Kansas City, purchased the ranch in 1988 after vacationing as guests for nearly 30 years. You too will want to come back.

C Lazy U Ranch
3640 Colorado Highway 125
PO Box 379
Granby, Colorado 80446
(970) 887-3344

Fresh Berry and Toasted Almond Salad

RASPBERRY VINAIGRETTE
Makes 3¼ cups

In a blender or food processor, combine raspberry puree, honey, and vinegar and whisk together until well blended. Add oil slowly, whisking until dressing is smooth and creamy. Add basil and continue to whisk for 1 minute or until well blended.

TO TOAST ALMONDS

Place almonds on a cookie sheet. Place in oven at 350 degrees for 4 minutes or until almonds turn golden brown. Set aside to cool.

TO ASSEMBLE SALAD

In a large bowl, toss salad greens and spinach with Raspberry Vinaigrette dressing, making sure all leaves are coated with the dressing. Place on a salad plate and top with fruit and almonds. Serve and enjoy.

 YIELD
Serves 12

½ bag mixed field greens

½ bag spinach

3 cups raspberry vinaigrette (recipe follows)

1 cup fresh strawberries

1 cup fresh blueberries

1 cup fresh raspberries

½ cup toasted almonds

RASPBERRY VINAIGRETTE

¾ cup raspberry puree (fresh or frozen raspberries)

½ cup honey

¾ cup champagne vinegar

¼ cup fresh basil, chopped

1 cup olive oil

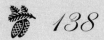

4 ounces smoked salmon

8 ounces cream cheese

2 ounces lemon juice

¼ cup fresh herbs, chopped
    (basil, oregano, thyme)

salt and pepper to taste

1 cucumber, sliced about
    ¼ inch thick

capers for garnish

Smoked Salmon on a Cucumber Chip

In a food processor, add cream cheese and blend until smooth. Add salmon until well blended. Add lemon juice and herbs and season with salt and pepper to taste.

Using a pastry bag and small tip, pipe out filling onto cucumber chips.

For garnish, add two capers to each cucumber chip. Store refrigerated or serve immediately.

YIELD
Serves 12

Pancetta-Onion Stuffed Pork Chops

Sauté onion for 4 minutes or until translucent. Combine onion, cheese, and pancetta. Season with salt and pepper. Cut a small pocket in chop and stuff with mixture. Grill chop and then finish in oven. Serve with balsamic glaze (recipe follows).

BALSAMIC GLAZE

Sauté vegetables until golden. Deglaze pan with vinegar and reduce the glaze to 2 cups. Add water and reduce by one-third more. Whisk in sugar and season to taste. Strain and serve on pork.

YIELD
Serves 1

one 10-ounce center-cut
   pork chop

½ red onion, sliced

1 ounce pancetta, cut into
   small cubes

1 ounce Port Salut cheese, cubed

salt and pepper to taste

BALSAMIC GLAZE

1 white onion, coarsely chopped

2 stalks celery, chopped

1 large carrot, chopped

3 cups balsamic vinegar

1 cup water

1 cup sugar

salt and pepper to taste

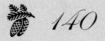

eight 8-ounce airline chicken
breasts (boneless breast
with wing attached)

fresh herbs (basil, oregano,
thyme, parsley)

salt and pepper to taste

SAUCE

1 quart chicken stock or chicken
base

10 garlic cloves

½ cup dried chilies, chopped
(Anaheim, poblano,
or red chili)

½ cup fresh herbs, chopped

½ pound butter, cubed

2 tablespoons olive oil

C Lazy U's Roasted Chicken

Season chicken. Sear on a flat-top grill or in a sauté pan until golden brown. Finish chicken in oven at 350 degrees for 20 minutes.

SAUCE

Drizzle garlic cloves with olive oil and roast in oven for 25 minutes. Strain oil and save for future sautéing.

Add everything in a pot. Bring to a boil and then reduce for 1 hour on medium heat. Finish sauce by whisking in butter. Ladle over chicken. Serve with rice or roasted potato.

YIELD

Serves 8

Strawberries-and-Cream Tart

TART SHELL (MAKES 12¾ OUNCES DOUGH)

Cream butter and sugar together until light. Add egg and blend well. Add flour and mix on low speed until fully incorporated. Chill for 30 minutes.

Roll out dough until it is 1 inch bigger than a 12-inch pan. Place in pan. Remove excess dough from edges and bake at 375 degrees until the shell is pale golden.

FILLING (FOR A 12-INCH TART)

Beat cream cheese until soft and then spread in baked tart shell. Mash strawberries to measure 1 cup. Mix sugar and cornstarch in saucepan. Stir in water and mashed strawberries. Cook on medium heat, stirring constantly until it boils. Boil 1 minute.

Fill shell with sliced strawberries. Pour cooked strawberry mixture over the sliced strawberries to cover completely. Refrigerate until set, about 3 hours.

Cut into 12 slices. Garnish with whipped cream, fresh mint, and chocolate sauce on plate.

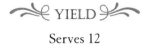

YIELD
Serves 12

TART SHELL (MAKES 12¾ OUNCES DOUGH)

8 tablespoons unsalted butter

¼ cup granulated sugar

½ egg

1¼ cups flour

FILLING (FOR A 12-INCH TART)

4 ounces cream cheese

6 cups fresh strawberries, sliced

1 cup granulated sugar

3 tablespoons cornstarch

½ cup cold water

DEVIL'S THUMB RANCH

Long before the white man came and fought over the gold and silver in this part of the Continental Divide, the Native Americans fought over the land itself. Arapaho and Ute contested for the right to live and hunt this area, but eventually decided to settle their differences. Legend says that they finally buried the Devil but left his thumb exposed to remind themselves of the evils that war brought. Today this rocky outcropping is a prominent feature of the ranch that took its name from the legend.

Both the Ute and the Arapaho continued to live in the area until white men invaded it to look for precious metals. As settlers and miners arrived, they tended to regard the Indians as unimportant to their objectives, even though they had lived in the mountains and valleys for hundreds of years. But in recognition of the Indians' presence, the settlers often identified things using Native American words. The town of Tabernash is named after a Ute chief who was killed nearby in 1878.

Traffic through the area was common, with people always headed to or from a real or imagined gold or silver strike. The stagecoach route that began in what was then called Idlewild, but today is Winter Park, passed through the ranch land along the Fawn Creek Trail. The stagecoach was eventually replaced by the railroad that arrived in 1904. Despite the decline in the demand for and the value of silver after the 1893 crash, the trains continued to bring more people to Colorado seeking fortunes and opportunity. The land was rich agriculturally, and where mines were of little value, high mountain plains were used for cattle grazing.

In the 1930s, Margaret Radcliff recognized how cattle thrived in the area. She built the original ranch homestead specifically to operate it as a dairy. It was her brothers—Dan, Louis, and George Yager—who turned Devil's Thumb Ranch into a vacation property in 1946. They eventually incorporated the Radcliff homestead into the ranch facilities, and the original building exists today as the Ranch House Saloon.

The Yagers operated the ranch as both a working ranch and dude ranch until the 1970s, when they introduced cross-country skiing in the winter of 1975. The current owners, Bob and Suzanne Fanch, purchased the ranch in 2001 to save it from developers who planned to fill the valley with residences and a golf course. The Fanches immediately began making improvements to the facilities but were determined to affect the land as little as possible.

The original homestead building for the ranch, which dates to the early 1930s, was restored and expanded. It now houses the Ranch House Restaurant, which offers truly elegant meals. Sixteen ridgetop cabins were added, along with a new 53-room lodge. And still, the footprint of man is a minor mark on the beauty of the valley, with buildings occupying only 2 percent of the property. The rest of the land is carefully supervised by the ranch's own forestry expert and his staff. They have been so successful in maintaining a natural environment that it is not unusual for them to share their mountain fishing pond with a moose.

The ranch's transformation also includes installation of the state's most comprehensive geothermal heating system, which—along with several other "green" programs—has earned the owners two environmental and responsible development awards. Guest cabins, the main building activities center, and the spa and swimming pool are all heated by the warm waters pumped up from hundreds of feet below the earth's surface. It is a never-ending supply of the cleanest energy available to man.

Devil's Thumb Ranch is open year-round and affords guests a unique environmentally sensitive, rustically fashionable wilderness resort experience amidst 4,000 acres of flowering meadows and lush woodlands. It is perhaps one of the most elegant dude ranches in America.

Devil's Thumb Ranch
3530 County Road 83
PO Box 750
Tabernash, Colorado 80478
(800) 933-4339

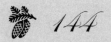
VINAIGRETTE

½ cup honey

2 tablespoons poppy seeds

¼ cup sherry vinegar

¾ cup extra virgin olive oil

7 cups baby spinach

3 peaches, pits removed,
    sliced thin

6 tablespoons toasted
    sunflower seeds

salt and pepper

Salad of Local Spinach and Colorado Peaches
with Honey–Poppy Seed Vinaigrette

VINAIGRETTE

Heat honey and poppy seeds in a small saucepan until you see three bubbles. Remove from heat and let it stand for 5 minutes. Whisk in sherry vinegar and then olive oil. Season with salt and pepper.

In a large mixing bowl, toss spinach and sunflower seeds together. Then add the vinaigrette to coat the spinach leaves. Season with salt and pepper.

Place your dressed greens on a plate and place the sliced peaches atop the greens.

 YIELD

Serves 6

Rib Eye Marinated in Brown Sugar, Bourbon, and Rosemary

Combine brown sugar, bourbon, and rosemary in a mixing bowl. It will be the consistency of a loose paste. Dredge the rib eyes in this mixture and marinate at least 4–5 hours before grilling. Grill to desired doneness.

YIELD
Serves 6

6 bone-in 12- to 14-ounce rib eyes

1½ cups brown sugar

1½ cups bourbon (your choice; the chef uses Jim Beam)

½ cup chopped rosemary

Pan-Seared Millbrook Farm Venison

Season venison loins with salt and pepper. Over medium heat, add the olive oil to a large sauté pan and sear the venison on both sides. Cook in a 350-degree oven until desired doneness.

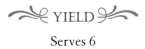
YIELD
Serves 6

six 5-ounce portions of venison loin

3 tablespoons olive oil

salt and pepper

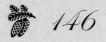
4 ears of corn, shucked and cut off the cob; reserve cobs

3 cups heavy cream

8 egg yolks

Sweet Corn Flan

Add corn, cobs, and heavy cream and bring to a boil. When corn is tender, puree and pass through a fine sieve. Measure the volume of this puree. Use a ratio of 10 egg yolks to 1 quart of corn cream. Mix in the egg yolks and bake the flan in a ramekin in a water bath until set. Bake at 350 degrees for 30–45 minutes.

❧ YIELD ❧
Serves 6

"Winter Park is a pivotal point in the history of skiing in Colorado. This is a very, very holy place."

—John Prosser, Professor of Architecture, University of Colorado

GRAND LAKE LODGE

For thousands of years, travelers to Grand Lake have marveled at the abundance of wildlife, game, and fish as well as timber, breathtaking views, and precious minerals. Paleo-Indians were the first visitors to the area in search of game and maybe even mammoths, which they found in the rugged glacial valleys near Grand Lake.

Indian warriors, fur trappers, mountain men, and gold miners traversed the area. In the 1800s Cheyenne, Sioux, and Arapaho Indians searched the area for bison and big game. The Grand River Utes and the other tribes fought ferocious battles that led to "the Legend of Spirit Lake." By 1879 the Utes of Middle Park had all been moved west, and soon the other tribes disappeared from the region.

French trappers seeking beaver pelts made early maps, while explorers later arrived while seeking the source of the Colorado River, known as the "Grand River" until 1921. Grand Lake in Grand County, Colorado, is the beginning of the river, which then flows through Grand Junction, Grand Mesa, and the Grand Dike. It extends past Moab, Utah, and into Canyonlands National Park in Utah. The river runs through the Grand Canyon of Arizona. John Fremont, "Pathfinder of the West," arrived in Middle Park in 1844, only to be ambushed by 200 Sioux and Arapaho braves. In 1854 a Scottish baron—Sir George Gore, whose name graces the Gore Range to the southwest of Grand Lake—traveled with the famous guide, Jim Bridger. Unfortunately, history records Gore as the one who slaughtered deer, sheep, elk, bear, antelope, and buffalo by the thousands.

Renowned explorer John Wesley Powell visited the area in 1868 and scaled Longs Peak. William Henry Jackson mapped the Grand River's source. The first photograph of Grand Lake was taken by Jackson in 1874. The Hayden Survey Party slept at the cabin of Judge Wescott, the first permanent resident of the area and a noted hunter and fisherman.

After the Colorado gold rush in 1859, when the phrase "Pike's Peak or Bust!" originated, access to Grand Lake was difficult until wagon roads at the passes were cut. In the 1870s and 1880s gold, silver, lead, and copper were discovered nearby. Soon shops, hotels, and saloons were built for entertainment and comfort.

After the county seat was moved from Hot Sulphur Springs to Grand Lake in 1881, the rival politicos had a deadly shoot-out on July 4, 1883. Four men perished, including the county clerk and three county commissioners. Later, the deputy may have been murdered by a posse near Utah. The sheriff, who later committed suicide, brought the death toll to six. Soon the end of the mining era

and frightened new investors brought hard times to the area. By 1890 the population was down to just 80, from a previous 600. Even the county seat moved.

Yet, in the summer of 1900, there were 1,000 residents and the area boomed. Wealthy folks from Denver and adjacent states arrived by stagecoach to build lavish cabins by the lake. In 1912 the World's Highest Yacht Club was built; and Sir Thomas Lipton, the tea baron, donated the Lipton Cup to the club.

President Teddy Roosevelt's Conservation Movement helped to protect the natural beauty. By 1918 over 150,000 tourists had enjoyed Rocky Mountain National Park, the nation's tenth national park. Roe Emery, the father of Colorado tourism, envisioned an affordable circle tour of the Rockies. His vision was overextended, and he never got to finish the lodge that would complete his mountain dynasty.

In April 1919, the Grand Lake Lodge was begun by A. D. Lewis with the use of native lodgepole pine. Within a year, 100 buildings were finished. Then, in 1923, Roe Emery took control of the lodge from Lewis and successfully operated it for 30 years. Famous visitors, such as Henry Ford, enjoyed the view. Emery sold the empire to T. J. Manning of Denver. In 1963, I. B. and Ted James, two brothers from Nebraska, secured the area as private property. In 1993 the Grand Lake Lodge became a registered National Historic Landmark—a proud achievement for the four generations that have owned and operated the lodge. The Main Lodge serves fantastic food and embraces its historic past.

Grand Lake Lodge
PO Box 569
15500 US Highway 34 or
724 Grand Avenue
Grand Lake, Colorado 80447
(970) 627-3967

French Onion Soup

Sauté onions in a heavy saucepan on high heat for 30 minutes until golden brown. Add spices and cook for 2 minutes. Add brandy and flambé until alcohol is burned off. Add beef broth and cook for 1 hour on medium heat. Add salt and pepper to taste.

Cool and refrigerate until ready to use. To serve, bring soup to desired temperature. Ladle into ovenproof soup crocks or bowls, top with large croutons, and cover croutons with provolone or Swiss cheese. Place bowls of soup in the oven and broil until the cheese is browned and bubbly. Serve immediately.

8 yellow onions, julienned

½ tablespoon marjoram

½ tablespoon basil

½ tablespoon thyme

2 quarts beef bouillon

1 cup brandy

salt and pepper to taste

provolone or Swiss cheese, sliced

croutons

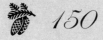

Sautéed Pork Loin Medallions with Crabmeat

6 ounces pork loin, cut into
3 medallions

½ cup flour

salt and white pepper to taste

1 ounce clarified butter

SAUCE

1 ounce clarified butter

1 ounce shitake mushrooms

1 shallot, finely diced

1–1½ ounces jumbo lump
crabmeat

3 ounces heavy whipping cream

2 ounces cooking sherry

salt and pepper to taste

parsley, finely chopped

Lightly pound each pork medallion until even and thin. Pat each side in flour and season with salt and pepper. In a medium sauté pan, add clarified butter until hot, not smoking. Gently place the pork medallions in the sauté pan and cook until lightly brown on both sides and cooked through, about 1 to 2 minutes on each side. Place medallions on plate and reserve.

SAUCE

In the same pan you used for cooking the pork medallions, add clarified butter and shitake mushrooms. Sauté until mushrooms begin to tenderize, about 1 to 2 minutes. Add the shallot and cook for another 30 seconds. Carefully add the cooking sherry to the mushroom mixture and let reduce by half once again, another 1 to 2 minutes. Add the heavy cream and reduce slowly until the mixture begins to thicken. Fold in the crabmeat and adjust the flavor with salt and pepper. Add chopped parsley for color and pour the sauce directly over the pork medallions. Serve immediately.

Sesame Seared Salmon

In a medium saucepan add olive oil, ginger, and garlic. Sauté over medium heat for 2 to 5 minutes until the ginger and garlic release their flavor. Add all liquid ingredients and cook over medium heat for 15 to 20 minutes. Add sugar and cook for another 5 to 10 minutes until fully dissolved. Make slurry (cornstarch and water) to thicken mixture slightly; ¼ cup should be enough. Cook 2 minutes and remove from heat; strain and cool properly.

In a medium sauté pan, place over medium heat and add olive oil blend. Coat one or both sides of the salmon fillet with black and white sesame seeds (one color of seeds is fine). Place gently into sauté pan and cook over medium heat for 1 to 2 minutes per side, until both sides are seared and the seeds form a crust. Place salmon in a preheated oven at 350 degrees and cook until desired, from 3 to 5 minutes. Keep sauté pan hot and add 2 ounces of teriyaki sauce to the pan. Add chopped cilantro, squeeze juice from lime wedge, and finish with the chopped scallions. Pour over salmon and serve.

6 ounces salmon fillet

black and white sesame seeds

olive oil

TERIYAKI SAUCE
(MAKES 2 CUPS)

1 tablespoon olive oil

3 tablespoons chopped
    ginger root

2 tablespoons chopped garlic

1 cup light soy sauce

½ cup granulated sugar

1 tablespoon brown sugar

½ cup pineapple juice

½ cup orange juice

cilantro, chopped

scallions, finely chopped

lime wedge

HOT SPRINGS LODGE & POOL

The Yampah Hot Springs was considered a sacred healing spot by the Ute Indians for hundreds of years before being discovered in 1860 by white settlers. Their word *Yampah* means "big medicine." Superheated waters have filtered up through the layers of sandstone into underground caves and pools of water for centuries.

A party of geographic explorers led by Captain Richard Sopris came to the area and quickly realized the value of the hot, mineral-rich waters. Twenty years later, Walter Devereux, his brothers Horace and James, and a group of British investors bought the Yampah Hot Springs and 10 acres of surrounding land. They set out to build the largest hot springs pool in the world in the newly established town of Glenwood Springs.

The first pool was finished in 1888. Known as the Natatorium, it was 615 feet long, 75 feet wide, and had a large fountain at one end. In 1890, a red sandstone bathhouse and lodge was built at a cost of $100,000. Designed by Austrian architect Theodore von Rosenberg, the bathhouse was fitted with special accommodations for pool bathing, tubs, and Roman vapor baths.

The walls of both the pool and the bathhouse were of solid masonry peachblow sandstone quarried from nearby mines. Each of the building's 44 bathrooms included a separate dressing and lounging room. The building also contained smoking and reading rooms, a physician's office, a ladies' parlor, and a gymnasium. It wasn't long before word of this unique new resort spread. Visitors from around the world arrived by train, and they included European royalty, U.S. senators, presidents, and movie stars.

The Hotel Colorado construction began in 1892 during the height of the silver boom. It was completed the following year, and the two properties were linked by the owner, Walter Devereux.

The practice of using mineral water to treat or cure diseases is called balneology. Like the Native Americans before them, wealthy visitors use the hot mineral baths to increase their body temperature, thus killing harmful germs and viruses, eliminating toxins, increasing their blood flow and circulation, and increasing their metabolism. The 3.5 million gallons of hot, mineral-rich water that flow through this bath system daily offer every opportunity for anyone who believes in mineral water healing.

People were so convinced of the healing powers of these 120-degree waters that many came to Colorado just to soak their bodies and absorb the minerals. Doc Holliday, who suffered from tuberculosis for many years, came to Glenwood Springs just to ease his pain. His untimely death did not discourage others from coming.

During WWII the U.S. Navy, which had established a hospital in the nearby Hotel Colorado, used the pools for therapeutic purposes. Navy doctors felt that this treatment was important for emotionally and physically disabled sailors and marines. During this period, the pool was closed to the public.

After the war, the bathhouse was converted to a private hospital called the Glenwood Clinic. As the need for the clinic declined, the building was converted again into a hotel, called Hot Springs Lodge. Renovations to the pool included a children's wading pool, water slide, miniature golf, and a new filtration system. As business grew, a new lodge was built next door, and the old stone bathhouse was also renovated to contain the snack bar, athletic club, conference facilities, and administrative offices.

Hot Springs Lodge & Pool is a blend of the past and present. Modern shower facilities and a state-of-the-art, ozone pool purification system maximize visitors' enjoyment as they relax in the hot mineral spring waters that continuously filter up through layers of sandstone from deep in the earth.

Hot Springs Lodge & Pool
PO Box 308
Glenwood Springs, Colorado 81602
(800) 537-7946
(970) 945-6571

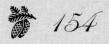

Banana Nut Bread

10 ounces margarine

3 cups granulated sugar

5 eggs

3 cups bananas, mashed

4 cups all-purpose flour

¼ cup baking powder

2 teaspoons salt

½ teaspoon baking soda

1 cup pecans or walnuts, chopped

¾ cup milk

Cream margarine and sugar on medium speed for 5 minutes, using flat beater.

Add eggs to creamed mixture. Beat 2 minutes. Add bananas and beat 1 minute.

Combine dry ingredients and nuts. Add dry ingredients and milk to creamed mixture. Mix on low speed for 1 minute.

Divide batter among four greased loaf pans (5 by 9 by 2¾ inches). Bake at 350 degrees for 50 minutes. Cut into 16 slices per loaf.

YIELD
Makes four 5-by-9-inch loaves

Cheesecake

CRUST

Combine crumbs, sugar, and melted margarine. Place 1 cup crumb mixture into each of three 8-inch pie pans or three 6-by-6-inch square cake pans. Press crumbs onto sides and bottoms of pans.

Let cream cheese stand until it reaches room temperature. Cream until smooth using flat beater. Add eggs slowly to cream cheese while beating. Add sugar and vanilla to cheese mixture. Beat on high speed for about 5 minutes. Place about 3 cups filling in each shell. Bake at 350 degrees for 30–35 minutes or until set. Do not overbake.

TOPPING

Mix sour cream, ¼ cup sugar, and vanilla. Spread 1 cup topping on each cake.

Sprinkle with a few graham cracker crumbs. Bake 10 minutes.

YIELD
Makes 3 cakes

CRUST

1½ cups graham cracker crumbs

¾ cup granulated sugar

¾ cup margarine, melted

FILLING

36 ounces cream cheese

6 eggs

1 cup granulated sugar

1 tablespoon vanilla

TOPPING

3 cups sour cream

¼ cup granulated sugar

1 teaspoon vanilla

¼ cup graham cracker crumbs

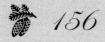

one 7-inch unbaked pizza crust

2 tablespoons salsa

1 large egg, beaten

¼ cup your choice of meat
    (bacon, ham, sausage)

cheddar cheese

Breakfast Pizza

Press center of pizza dough to create reservoir for ingredients. Spread salsa and beaten egg over pizza. Add your choice of meat, and top with shredded cheddar cheese.

Bake at 375 degrees for 10 minutes—until egg is cooked through and cheese is melted.

"I feel a recipe is only a theme, which an intelligent cook can play each time with a variation."

—Madame Benoit

HOTEL BRISTOL

For almost 60 years, the Hotel Bristol has been an icon in Steamboat Springs. However in December of 1971, when Andy Van Baak walked into nearby Ski Time Square for a job interview, all he saw was mud-slicked streets. Thankfully he drove two miles west, found Steamboat Springs, and was awestruck. Andy landed an entry-level job—and in a twist of fate, and following years of experience as a controller for several of the local hotels, he became the owner of the Hotel Bristol.

Located at an elevation of 7,000 feet in downtown Steamboat Springs, the Hotel Bristol is an intimate, full-service hotel "the way it used to be." It features a restaurant and saloon right on the premises, serving up pasta and pizza and libations to quench the thirst of any real or weekend cowboy. There's off-street parking for your iron steed and a free city shuttle just out the front door to whisk you to all the wonders of Steamboat Springs.

In 1948 the police chief of Steamboat Springs, Everett Bristol, took advantage of access to building materials not available during WWII—as did many other citizens throughout the country. The new hotel bore its builder's name.

As the Hotel Bristol matured, Harold and Irene Killham took over as new owners and added a lobby and parking lot. Their family was to guide the hotel's direction for the next quarter century, managed by daughter and son-in-law Joan and Sam Graione. Almost overnight, the Steamboat Springs ski area changed the Bristol from a hotel where visiting businessmen took pleasure in Irene Killham's homemade pies to an in-demand lodge for the region's invasion of seasonal visitors. Both Frontier and Continental airlines helped bring 200,000 winter skiers to a town with a total of only 1,000 available rooms.

Following the Killham family's departure, the 1980s saw a succession of Hotel Bristol owners. In 1994, after spending many years studying area hotels, Andy Van Baak purchased the hotel and changed its name to Clermont Inn Bed & Breakfast. He hired manager Tonya Dean, and they worked together to revitalize the new bed and breakfast.

At one time in the 1950s, a pool hall was located on the ground floor. Throughout the 1960s, the ground floor was used by geologists who studied rocks taken from a nearby molybdenum mine. Today, Mazzola's restaurant has transformed the hotel's ground level into a popular dining room for both locals and tourists.

 *158*

In May of 1997, Andy renamed the Clermont as the Hotel Bristol to return it to its heritage. He and his wife, Arlene, redecorated the hotel to reflect the way things used to be in Steamboat Springs. Its 22 rooms are a tribute to Steamboat's past. And Mazzola's is still a gathering place for residents in the know.

Hotel Bristol
917 Lincoln Avenue
PO Box 774927
Steamboat Springs, Colorado 80477
(970) 879-3083

Seafood Lasagna

You can use your favorite marinara recipe or substitute store-bought marinara and Alfredo.

In a large pot, warm the half-and-half and heavy cream. Set aside until needed.

In a separate large pot, melt butter over medium-high heat. Add the garlic to the butter and sauté until cooked but not brown. Add the flour to the garlic-butter mixture and cook over low heat while stirring for 5 minutes.

Add the wine. Whisk in the warm cream mixture. Cook over medium heat, whisking constantly until the mixture coats the back of a spoon. Remove from heat, add 2 cups of Pecorino Romano cheese, and chill. Season to taste with salt and pepper.

LASAGNA

Grate the mozzarella, provolone, and Fontina cheese into a bowl. In a large skillet, heat oil over medium-high heat; add seafood and cook until the shrimp is no longer translucent. Remove from heat and chill.

Lay the pasta sheets out on a table and spread a third of the ricotta cheese on each sheet. Spread all of the marinara in the bottom of a 2-inch deep, 8-by-10-inch casserole dish. Set one of the cheesy pasta sheets in the pan, pour in a third of the Alfredo sauce, and sprinkle with

1 pound medium shrimp, peeled and cleaned

1 pound medium scallops, cleaned

2 tablespoons olive oil

1 cup marinara sauce

3 pasta sheets (enough fresh pasta to make three 8-by-10 sheets)

2 cups ricotta cheese

¼ cup mozzarella

¼ cup provolone

¼ cup Fontina cheese

4 cups Alfredo sauce (recipe follows)

½ cup chopped fresh basil

salt and pepper

ALFREDO SAUCE

½ stick butter

2 tablespoons flour

¼ cup chopped garlic

6 ounces white wine

2 cups half-and-half

2 cups heavy cream

2 cups Pecorino Romano cheese

salt and pepper to taste

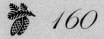

a third of the mozzarella cheese mixture, half of the seafood mix, and half of the basil. Season lightly with salt and pepper.

Place the second cheesy pasta sheet into the pan, pour in a third of the Alfredo sauce, and sprinkle with a third of the mozzarella cheese mixture, half of the seafood mix, and half of the basil. Season lightly with salt and pepper.

Lay the last cheesy pasta sheet into the pan and top with the remaining Alfredo and mozzarella mixture.

Cover with plastic wrap and then aluminum foil, and bake at 350 degrees for 90 minutes. Remove foil and plastic wrap and finish baking for 30 minutes. The internal temperature of the lasagna should be 165 degrees.

YIELD

Serves 12

Fresh Berries with Sabayon Sauce

For the egg mixture, combine the yolks, sugar, Amaretto, and vanilla in a medium mixing bowl. Heat over a water bath while whisking constantly until the mixture is warm and close to ribbon stage. Cool in refrigerator, stirring occasionally.

Place the cream, sugar, and vanilla in a mixer. Whip until stiff peaks form. Fold in the cooled egg mixture to create sabayon sauce. Refrigerate until needed.

Divide the berries among 12 bowls, and top with chilled sabayon sauce.

YIELD

Serves 12

2 egg yolks

¼ cup sugar

¼ cup Amaretto

½ teaspoon vanilla

1 cup heavy cream

1 tablespoon sugar

¼ teaspoon vanilla

2 quarts fresh berries or fruit, washed and cut if needed

HOTEL COLORADO

Following the onslaught of prospectors, miners, businessmen, investors, and the mass of humanity necessary to support them, Colorado had towns springing up everywhere. The discovery of gold and silver enticed even more people to come in search of fortune, and many stayed. It wasn't long before tourists began to venture here, and some people even came for their health.

Walter Devereux arrived in 1887 and discovered what the Ute Indians had known for centuries. Native Americans used the mineral springs along the Grand River (later named the Colorado River) for therapeutic purposes, calling them *Yampah*, meaning "big medicine." White settlers came in the 1880s, staking claims to the hot springs and hoping to profit from their healing powers.

Devereux purchased 10 acres around the undeveloped hot springs and began building. It only took a year to contain the 3 million gallons of 126-degree water in an elegant red sandstone bathhouse. Electric lighting for the project was expanded to include the town, and Glenwood Springs was the first city of its size in America to use electricity.

So many visitors arrived that Devereux decided he needed a hotel to accommodate them. Construction began in 1892 at the height of the silver boom, and the "Grand Dame of the Rockies" was completed in 1893 at a cost of $850,000. No expense was spared as Devereux erected two elaborate six-story towers that served as the focal point for the hotel. Built of local peachblow sandstone, Hotel Colorado mirrored the beauty of the surrounding red rock canyons.

More than 200 guest rooms offered indoor plumbing, electric lighting, and either steam heating or ornate fireplaces. Hydraulic elevators carried guests who chose not to climb the grand stairways. Victorian gardens surrounded the property, and the illuminated Florentine Fountain in the courtyard sprayed water 185 feet in the air—the highest fountain in the world. An elevated footbridge carried guests to the hot springs, where they could hope to improve their health.

In 1905, President Roosevelt camped at the hotel for 3 weeks, making forays into the local wilderness to hunt bears and mountain lions. On one particular day, he failed to bag any game at all. The industrious staff fashioned a stuffed bear that they had pieced together from scraps of material. His daughter fell in love with the gift and soon named it "Teddy." Thus was born one of the world's most enduring toys, the teddy bear.

The Hotel Colorado served as a playground to society's elite for many years. President Taft arrived in 1909 in a private train car. A parade of carriages carried Taft and his party to Hotel Colorado. When offered exclusive use of the hot springs pool he declined, saying, "I've found it's much better for a man of my size not to bathe in public." No one knew for sure how heavy he was, but he buried the needle on a scale that measured up to 360 pounds.

During the roaring '20s, the hotel became an attractive playground for Chicago gangsters such as Al Capone and the Verain Brothers, Bert and Jack (alias Diamond Jack Alterie). Armed with gun belts, Diamond Jack Alterie wore flashy diamonds in his rings, shirt studs, watches, and belt buckles. Surrounded by bodyguards, these big spenders arrived at the Hotel Colorado via large Lincoln convertibles.

The unsinkable Molly Brown got her nickname by surviving the sinking of the *Titanic*. And she got her wealth from her husband's abundant gold strike. Molly Brown visited Hotel Colorado to enjoy one of society's favorite playgrounds. One of the hotel's Tower Suites has been transformed into a living tribute to this dynamic woman of history.

In 1942 the U.S. Navy took over the hotel and hot springs, turning the complex into a military hospital. By the war's end, more than 6,500 patients had been admitted to the facility.

Over the years, the Hotel Colorado has undergone several renovations, name changes, and owners. Today it stands as an elegant tribute to the fascinating history of Colorado.

Hotel Colorado
526 Pine Street
Glenwood Springs, Colorado 81601
(800) 544-3998

Chocolate Epiphany

24 egg yolks

8 whole eggs

½ cup sugar

½ tablespoon salt

1 tablespoon vanilla

2 pounds butter

8 cups chocolate chips
(dark or semisweet)

This recipe was meant for small Bundt cake pans that hold six cakes per pan. However, you can be creative. We have used many different types of pans.

By hand, beat together the eggs, sugar, salt, and vanilla in a large bowl. Melt the butter and chocolate chips separately in the microwave. Add the melted butter to the egg mixture and beat well; then add the melted chocolate and keep beating by hand real hard, using a whisk. Always add the eggs first, then the butter, then the chocolate and beat with whisk.

When the batter is ready, generously spray the Bundt pans with cooking oil. Fill the pans and bake at 325 degrees for 8 minutes. Rotate the pans and bake for 8 more minutes. Cool the cakes on a rack. To avoid having cakes stick to the pan, hit each pan on a wooden table 3 or 4 times and then turn them upside down onto plastic wrap. Wrap the cakes individually. Keep them refrigerated.

YIELD
Makes 3 small Bundt cakes

Red Curry Chicken Soup

Note: Coconut milk and red curry paste can be found in an Asian or specialty food store. Busha Browne's Original Banana Chutney can be ordered from:

Busha Browne's Company Ltd.
697 Spanish Town Road
PO Box 332
Kingston 11, Jamaica W.I.
Website: bushabrowne.com

Sauté garlic in butter first, until golden and nutty; then add celery, carrots, and onion. Add chicken and toss with the veggies. Add red curry paste (1 tablespoon or more if you like spicy). Be careful—this stuff has kick!

Bring to a boil the coconut milk and chicken broth. Thicken up only a touch with roux. Strain into your veggies, chicken, and red curry paste mix. Bring to a simmer. Finish with cilantro.

When serving soup, garnish with a touch of banana chutney and a sprinkle of toasted coconut.

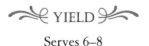

YIELD

Serves 6–8

1 tablespoon chopped garlic

2 tablespoons butter

½ cup diced celery

½ cup diced carrots

½ cup diced onion

1½ cups diced cooked chicken

1 tablespoon Mae Ploy red curry paste

3 cans (13.3 ounces) Chaokoh brand coconut milk from Thailand

2 cups chicken broth

½ cup fresh cilantro, chopped

1½ cups Busha Browne's Original banana chutney

sweetened, shredded coconut

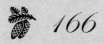

1 quart heavy cream

⅔ cup brown sugar

1 teaspoon vanilla extract

zest of 2 oranges, chopped fine

12 egg yolks

caramel sauce

Orange Crème Caramel

Scald the cream, sugar, vanilla, and orange zest. When this mixture scalds, temper the yolks by mixing them with a little of the hot mixture and then add the yolk mixture to the cream.

Spray custard cups with pan spray and place a little caramel sauce in the bottom of the cups. Fill the cups with custard and bake for 50 minutes, covered, in a water bath at 350 degrees.

HOTEL JEROME

During the Civil War a Union colonel, Jerome B. Wheeler, disobeyed an order and drove a supply wagon train through Confederate lines to relieve a surrounded and starving regiment. For this he was demoted to the rank of major; but most people, in particular the members of the regiment he saved, called him a hero of the war.

Wheeler married well after the war, and he was eventually brought into the department store business created by Rowland H. Macy when his brother-in-law inherited Macy's from Rowland's descendents. Amassing wealth quickly, Wheeler began investing in silver mines in Colorado in 1883—sight unseen. His focus was on a small area to the west of Leadville known as Aspen. Leadville had been the site of the first silver discovery in the area, so any mine nearby could be very valuable.

In 1887, Wheeler's partner bought out his share of Macy's, and Jerome Wheeler moved to Manitou Springs, Colorado, for his wife's health. Back then, Manitou Springs was referred to as "the Newport of the Rockies."

Jerome Wheeler had the money to live in luxury, surrounded by wealthy neighbors; but he was not content with resort living. He was drawn to the investments he had made in businesses and mining properties, which were in great abundance in the Aspen area. It was back in 1879 when the first prospectors arrived in the Roaring Fork Valley via treacherous Independence Pass, which crosses the Continental Divide at nearly 12,100 feet. Thirteen of them stayed the winter to protect their claims. They named the area Ute City after the Native Americans who had lived in the area for centuries.

In 1880, the mine owners laid out a town site and named it Aspen. After Wheeler began investing in the mining camp, other investors followed and the town prospered. By 1885, hydroelectric power, generated from Hunter Creek, was used in the mines, and it was extended to offer public electricity throughout the community.

In 1887 the railroad reached Aspen—the same year Wheeler came to live in Colorado. Progress was quick, largely due to the great abundance of silver discovered and the ease of getting it to smelters on railcars.

The year 1889 saw the construction of the Hotel Jerome as well as the Wheeler Opera House, both financed and built by Jerome Wheeler. They were and still are monuments to the great prosperity silver mining brought to the region. By 1892, Aspen had become the largest silver-producing district in the nation, supplying one-sixth of the United States' silver and one-sixteenth of the world's total.

It all unraveled quickly in 1893 when Congress repealed the Sherman Silver Act, which had made silver certificates redeemable for gold. Since it could no longer be converted to gold, the value of silver plunged, and many fortunes were greatly diminished. Mining activity slowed dramatically, but some mines remain active. The world's largest silver nugget, at 2,200 pounds, was discovered in the Smuggler Mine in 1894.

The Hotel Jerome survived even though Aspen's population fell from a peak of 12,000 to about 700 in the 1930s. In 1936, a new discovery would create a new destiny for Aspen and the Hotel Jerome. In a word, snow. Ski runs were mapped out and investors again flocked to the area. It became such a popular sport and was such a great location that Aspen held the first national downhill and slalom skiing championships in 1941. Even the U.S. Army's 10th Mountain Division came to the area to train that year.

Today, Wheeler is considered an Aspen icon primarily for the three buildings, still standing, that bear his name—the Wheeler/Stallard Museum, the Wheeler Opera House, and the Hotel Jerome. In the heart of downtown Aspen, Hotel Jerome was designed to be a paragon of hospitality for its day. The resort offers 92 richly appointed, uncommonly spacious guest rooms and suites, several restaurants, and the ever-popular J Bar with authentic saloon ambiance. Hotel Jerome's ornate Victorian mine-camp flavor has been painstakingly preserved and restored so that the smallest detail is a reflection of the whole.

Hotel Jerome
330 East Main Street
Aspen, Colorado 81611
(800) 253-3114
(970) 920-1000

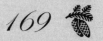

Mustard-Crusted Trout

Season the trout fillets with salt and pepper. Liberally brush Dijon mustard on the flesh side. Coat with the herb bread crumbs and refrigerate until ready to cook.

Pan-fry the trout until golden brown (about 2 minutes on each side, depending on the thickness of the trout) over medium-high heat. Add the tomatoes. Add the chopped sage. Add the lemon-chicken broth and bring to a boil.

Add the diced butter cubes and cook until the sauce has the consistency of gravy. Sauté the mushrooms in a separate pan. Add mushrooms to the trout. Garnish with the scallions and serve.

LEMON-CHICKEN BROTH
Combine broth and juice and heat to a boil; then remove from stove.

HERB BREAD CRUMBS
Combine all ingredients in the food processor and blend until the mixture turns green and the crumbs are very fine.

---

eight 3- to 4-ounce trout fillets, mustard crusted

Dijon mustard

1 cup red and gold tomatoes, diced ⅜ inch

1 tablespoon chopped sage

1 cup lemon-chicken broth (recipe follows)

5 tablespoons cold diced butter

2 cups wild mushrooms

3 tablespoons scallions, sliced thinly on the bias

herb bread crumbs (recipe follows)

LEMON-CHICKEN BROTH

2 cups chicken broth, no sodium

¼ cup fresh lemon juice

HERB BREAD CRUMBS

½ loaf fresh white bread, no crust

1½ quarts dried plain bread crumbs

2 cups chopped parsley

2 cups chopped chives

4 cups roughly chopped basil

½ cup grated lemon zest

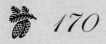

Cinnamon-Raisin Grits Bread

¼ ounce active dry yeast

1¼ cups warm water
(105 degrees)

2 tablespoons honey

2 tablespoons butter, soft

1 teaspoon salt

3 cups bread flour

½ cup cooked grits

2 teaspoons cinnamon

1 cup raisins

GLAZE

¾ cup powdered sugar

1–2 tablespoons milk

½ teaspoon vanilla extract

Activate the yeast with the water. Separately combine the butter, honey, salt, and grits with 2 cups of the flour. Add the yeast and mix for 1 minute. Knead the remainder of the flour by adding ½ cup at a time until the dough is smooth and not sticky.

Proof dough to double in size. Punch the dough down and knead in the cinnamon and raisins.

Shape the dough. Put it in a greased loaf pan and cover with oiled plastic wrap. Proof until double in size.

Bake at 375 degrees for 30–45 minutes or until the internal temperature is 190 degrees. You can glaze or use for French toast.

GLAZE
Mix all ingredients well.

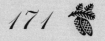

Seven-Grain and Nut Granola

Combine the first eight ingredients in a mixing bowl. In a saucepan, slowly heat the remaining ingredients until smooth and syrupy. Add to the dry ingredients and mix until evenly coated. On a parchment-lined sheet pan, gently spread out mixture in a ½-inch-thick layer. Then cook at 200 degrees, stirring every 8 minutes for 2 hours. Allow to cool completely. Crumble when finished and serve.

4 cups oatmeal

1 cup seven-grain cereal

½ cup almonds, sliced

½ cup hazelnuts, chopped

½ cup walnuts, chopped

½ cup pistachios

½ cup coconut, shredded

½ cup wheat germ

½ cup honey

½ cup butter, melted

1 tablespoon cinnamon

½ cup brown sugar

1 cup maple syrup

⅛ cup canola oil

¼ teaspoon nutmeg

¼ tablespoon salt

1 tablespoon vanilla extract

2 tablespoons water

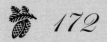

Trout Dip

2 cups small-diced onion

2 tablespoons sliced garlic

1 cup white wine

¼ cup Dijon mustard

1 tablespoon Worcestershire sauce

1 teaspoon Tabasco sauce

1 ounce fresh lemon juice

1 brick cream cheese

2 cups sour cream

2 tablespoons horseradish

Sauté onions and garlic over low heat until translucent and savory. Add Worcestershire, mustard, Tabasco, lemon juice, and wine. Cook until alcohol is evaporated (about 5 minutes) over medium-low heat.

Add the rest of the ingredients and mix gently to break up the cream cheese. Cool for service.

Serve warm or cold with crackers or toasted slices of French bread.

KEYSTONE LODGE & SPA

Summit County, located high in the Colorado Rockies, is known as Colorado's playground because of the numerous outdoor activities the area provides. The county is home to four major ski areas: Keystone, Copper Mountain, Breckenridge, and Arapahoe Basin. Organized as one of the 17 original Colorado counties by the First Territorial Legislature on November 1, 1861, Summit County was named for the many mountain summits in the area. Its boundaries have since been divided into seven counties.

The history of the Keystone Resort began in 1941 when Max Dercum purchased the Black Ranch (now known as Ski Tip Lodge) along the Snake River. He began to dream of a Keystone Ski Area. It took a while, but by 1949, Ski Tip Lodge had opened to overnight ski guests. It would remain open and continue to host innumerable guests over the next 63 years.

In the 1960s, Max Dercum and Bill Bergman actively pursued the development of Keystone Mountain with the vision of establishing an international ski area. In 1967, their dreams were realized when Keystone acquired more than 500 acres of land (470 from Wheaton College at a cost of $1.4 million and the remainder from private individuals). The ski area originally opened with just two lifts at the Keybase area (now known as the Mountain House Base Area), and two lodges, Keybase at the bottom and Keytop at the summit. Tens of thousands of skiers soon flocked to the new ski area for lift tickets costing only $5 per person.

The winter drought of 1976 was not a problem for Keystone which had fortuitously added snowmaking equipment in 1972. The price of $350,000 was high, but a worthwhile step that helped make the lodge an industry leader. It wasn't long before the resort began hosting annual events. One of these was a six-mile cross-country ski event called the Keystone Caper, which attracted 480 entrants. The Keystone Ranch Golf Course then opened, and Keystone gained a reputation as a service-oriented, family-style resort. A second 18-hole course along the river was opened in 2000.

From 1984 to 1994, the resort saw considerable expansion. The North Peak project totaled $15 million in installation and enhancements that included 12 new runs, two triple-chair lifts, and a gondola. Night skiing was made available, and the Keystone Lodge is now one of the largest night-skiing facilities in the world. Its Conference Center, accommodating up to 1,800 people, is the largest in the Rocky Mountain region. Two new quad lifts were installed in 1990, and The

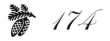

Outback opened with 300 acres for heli-skiing. A second gondola and two additional high-speed lifts were also opened.

By 1996, the Keystone Ski Patrol was chosen as the "Outstanding Alpine Ski Patrol" in the Rocky Mountain Division, and snowboarding was introduced with the opening of a new a snowboard park, complete with half-pipe and big hits. Additional snowshoeing and cross-country skiing trails give everyone an opportunity to work up an appetite.

Today, Keystone stretches 7 miles along the Snake River, over three mountains, and up to 3,128 vertical feet. It includes 3,148 acres of terrain and three villages with shops, stores, accommodations, bars, and restaurants. Find out for yourself why Max Dercum loved this area, and why one of the three mountains here is named after him.

Keystone Lodge & Spa
22101 US Highway 6
Keystone, Colorado 80435
(866) 455-ROCK
(970) 496-3000

Keystone Tuna

YUZU VINAIGRETTE

Combine shallots, honey, ginger juice, rice vinegar, and Yuzu juice. With a whisk, incorporate the oil; season with salt to taste.

SOY REDUCTION

Combine all ingredients in a saucepan over medium heat and reduce until they form a syrup. Strain and chill.

PASSION-FRUIT COULIS

Combine all ingredients in a saucepan over medium heat. Reduce by half and chill.

WATERMELON-CHILI WATER

Puree watermelon and sambal; strain through fine mesh strainer.

TO PLATE

Cut the avocados in half and slice thin. Form into a circle using four ring molds.

In a small bowl combine soba noodles, micro greens, and cooked lobster with a small amount of Yuzu vinaigrette, just to coat the salad. Place the salad in the middle of each avocado ring. Layer three pieces of sliced tuna on top of each salad, and top with the caviar. Drizzle some of the vinaigrette on the tuna before serving.

YUZU VINAIGRETTE

¼ cup fresh ginger juice

¼ cup rice vinegar

¼ cup Yuzu juice
(Japanese vinegar)

¼ cup honey

½ teaspoon minced shallots

1 cup of olive oil

SOY REDUCTION

2 cups low-sodium soy sauce

1 cup brown sugar

3 oranges, juiced, and the zest

½ cup mirin (Japanese cooking wine)

1 small piece sliced ginger

1 stalk lemongrass, minced

½ stick cinnamon

1 star anise

½ cup rice vinegar

PASSION-FRUIT COULIS

2 cups passion-fruit juice

1 cup sugar

WATERMELON-CHILI WATER

3 ounces fresh watermelon

¼ teaspoon sambal
(garlic chili paste)

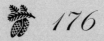

OTHER INGREDIENTS

twelve 1-ounce portions sushi-grade tuna (preferably bigeye from Hawaii)

2 ounces cooked lobster

¼ ounce cooked soba noodles

micro basil, to taste

micro shiso, to taste

2 avocados

farm-raised Osetra caviar, to taste

Drizzle the soy reduction sauce first on the plate, and then drizzle the passion-fruit coulis. Just before serving, spoon some of the watermelon-chili water around the plate.

YIELD

Serves 4

Warm Chocolate Lava Cake

Melt together, in a bowl over boiling water, the chocolate and the butter.

In an electric mixer, mix the eggs, yolks, port or liqueur, and vanilla extract until smooth. When chocolate and butter are melted, add to the egg mixture. When the mixture is smooth, sift in the flour and the powdered sugar. Scoop 3 ounces of the cake mix into 4-ounce buttered and floured ramekins. Chill completely.

Bake at 425 degrees for 8 minutes. Let rest for 1 to 2 minutes and remove from ramekins. Serve with your favorite ice cream.

10 ounces dark chocolate

10 ounces butter

3 tablespoons port wine or favorite liqueur

1 tablespoon vanilla extract

1 cup flour

¾ cup powdered sugar

5 whole eggs

2½ ounces egg yolk

Cheddar Cheese Lavosh

1 cup all-purpose flour

½ teaspoon salt

½ teaspoon finely ground black
pepper

1 cup shredded cheddar cheese

¼ cup olive oil

½ cup water

olive oil

sea salt

In your small Kitchen Aid mixer, with the dough hook, mix the dry ingredients. Add the cheese and the oil and let mix for 1–2 minutes. Slowly add the water until the dough forms a ball and pulls away from the sides of the bowl. If dough begins to work the mixer too much, finish by hand.

Roll the dough out until it is paper-thin. Brush the top with olive oil and sprinkle with sea salt. Bake at 350 degrees until golden brown.

Champagne Orchid Granita

Place all ingredients except for the orchid petals together in a saucepan and bring to a simmer. Remove from the heat and cool in a shallow baking dish. Chiffonade the orchid petals. (This is done by stacking leaves, rolling them tightly, and then cutting across the rolled leaves with a sharp knife, producing fine ribbons.)

When mixture is cool, add the orchid petals and place in the freezer. Every 20 minutes, take a fork and mix and crush the mixture. The mixture will begin to take on the appearance of a snow cone, or shaved ice. Keep this up for 3 to 4 hours until the mixture is light and fluffy.

Enjoy with fresh berries or just by itself.

"A gourmet is just a glutton with brains."

—Philip W. Haberman

1½ quarts water

2 cups sugar

1 bottle (750 ml.) champagne

5 whole star anise

10–12 orchids, petals removed and set aside

LARAMIE RIVER RANCH

Fur trappers and traders preceded the settlers in Larimer County. They competed with the local Indians for game until realizing they could trade for the pelts. The French had made claim to the area, and by treaty, thus eliminating any occasional influence the Spanish explorers might have had. But the land was brought under U.S. ownership when Napoleon was obligated to sell the Louisiana Purchase for $15 million to fund his war efforts in Europe.

While several well-publicized expeditions came to Colorado, such as one led by Zebulon Pike, it was trappers who named the Thompson River. There was no gold or silver to be found in the area; but the high mountain plains were suitable for ranching, which flourished.

The Laramie River Ranch was originally known as the UT Bar. The ranch dates back to 1880 when Tex Allen bought part of the ranch where the present buildings are situated and named it Horse Ranch. One of the original buildings, with its dirt roof, still stands. Daniel Johnson bought the place from Tex Allen and built a low, rambling house that was the scene of many country parties and dances. When the house burned, neighbors helped Mr. Johnson built a two-story house that, with a great deal of remodeling and additions, is now the main ranch house.

In 1897 Harry Tatham, who came to this country from England at the age of 15, bought the ranch from Johnson. The Tatham family ran the ranch as a cow-calf operation. When renovations were done in 1996, charred rock and bits of burned wood from the fire were found under the floorboards. Renovations of the walls upstairs revealed letters written to Susie Tatham from her sister and friends in Laramie. In addition to the letters, a number of newspapers dating to 1892 were found pasted to the walls for insulation.

Tom Tatham bought the ranch from his father in 1912. In the early years, Tom, like all the other ranchers, had trouble with the wolves. One especially—Old Two Toes, a killer wolf whose skull is now in Washington in a museum, was responsible for the loss of many cattle. Although Tom belled a number of his cows to scare the wolves, Old Two Toes soon got used to the bells. Tom started sleeping in a haystack, hoping to get a shot at him. The wolf wandered the country from Sand Creek to North Park, leaving a bloody trail of devastation and loss, until he was finally caught in a trap by Rattlesnake Jack.

Tom Tatham sold the ranch to Nelle and Rick Leake in 1929. They continued to run it as a cow-calf operation. The UT Bar name and brand were sold with the ranch. "It was chosen for its simplicity and the ease with which it can be applied and recognized." Brands are assigned by state, and it is interesting to note that the very same brand is registered across the border near Laramie—which must have made for some confusion at the stock yards.

In 1937, Nelle and Rick began accepting guests. As business picked up, Rick hired a skilled log man to construct five cabins. Nelle taught school for her daughter and the valley kids. At first, she held school in what is today the workshop. Later, the Leakes donated a parcel of land, and the Gleneyre School was built.

Before power arrived in the valley, Rick cut ice from the Laramie and put it in the ice house. Packed in sawdust and with the sod roof for insulation, the ice lasted all summer without melting. In addition to the ice house, the ranch had a "meat house." It was a low building, built right down on the river in the corner by the lodge where there is a little island of sorts. The water flowed through the building and kept the meat at a cool temperature while it was left to cure.

The ranch kept dairy cows and chickens to supply dairy products for the ranch. Once a week or so, guests and a crew member would get ice from the ice house, skim the cream from the day's milk, and get sugar from the kitchen. The ingredients were combined in an old hand-crank ice cream maker to produce dessert for that evening's meal. Homesteaders planted gardens out of necessity. Rhubarb was a symbol of homesteading because it provided much-needed fruit and vitamin C. In 1995 a small patch of rhubarb still grew near the river. Even today, fresh strawberry and rhubarb pie is served to the guests.

In 1944, Dr. and Mrs. Fred F. Snider from Chicago became partners in the business. Fred was a dentist, and his most famous referral was one of his patients—Hugh Downs, who hunted antelope on the ranch.

The Mink House (which stands today) was one of Fred's get-rich-quick projects. Fred was convinced that mink would be a wonderful way to supplement the ranch's income. Mink are carnivores, and there were plenty of old horses in the area. The project lasted just one season because the pelts brought only a small fraction of the price they expected. Also, the process of slaughtering the horses and feeding the nasty little animals was unpleasant. The remaining mink were released, and their offspring are still occasionally glimpsed on the ranch.

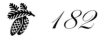

The ranch was eventually sold and passed through a succession of owners until Bill and Krista Burleigh bought it in 1995. They had to change the name from UT Bar because the brand did not transfer along with ownership of the ranch. Also, the new owners felt that the name Laramie River Ranch was both more descriptive and memorable. The full range of dude ranch activities are available today in this valley, which inspired the book and movie, *My Friend Flicka*.

The Laramie River Ranch is located in north central Colorado, just 6 miles from the Wyoming border. The high mountain passes close in winter, leaving valley residents isolated from the rest of Colorado. This makes Laramie, Wyoming, 42 miles away, their "local" community as well as their postal address.

Laramie River Ranch
25777 County Road 103
Jelm, Wyoming 82063
(800) 551-5731
(970) 435-5716

Sumptuous Cinnamon Rolls

Heat milk and oil until very warm—not hot enough to burn your finger. In a large bowl, combine half of the flour, sugar, salt, and yeast. Stir to blend well. Add warm liquid to flour mixture and beat with mixer, then add eggs and beat until moist. Add remaining flour while beating until the dough is elastic and sticky, but not so it sticks to fingers when pushed into the dough. Dough should feel soft and light to the touch—not too stiff. If you add too much flour, the rolls will be tough and not light and fluffy. Place dough in bowl sprayed with cooking oil and let rise in a warm place for about an hour, until doubled in size. Turn out on a lightly floured board, knead for a few minutes, and roll into a 10-by-8-inch rectangle about 1 inch thick. Spread softened margarine or butter across the entire surface of the dough. Sprinkle lightly with ground cinnamon, brown sugar, and chopped pecans. Roll up tightly like a jelly roll, starting at the long edge. Cut 2-inch thick slices with a sharp knife or kitchen string. Butter a large cake pan and sprinkle it with a thin layer of brown sugar. Place rolls cut side up in pan; let rise until double. Bake 20–30 minutes in preheated oven at 350 degrees until lightly golden brown.

These rolls are best hot out of the oven, but they can be stored and reheated with good results (to freeze, cool

3¾ cups milk

6 tablespoons vegetable oil or melted butter

3 tablespoons dry yeast (1 envelope = 1 tablespoon)

6 tablespoons sugar

1 teaspoon salt or less

2 beaten eggs

10 cups white flour or more as needed

brown sugar

chopped pecans

margarine or butter

ground cinnamon

FROSTING

½ pound margarine

6 cups powdered sugar

½ cup orange juice

1 cup condensed milk or half-and-half

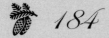

and wrap in tin foil). Some people like them served with a pat of butter or with frosting (recipe follows).

FROSTING

Mix with hand mixer and add enough milk to achieve the desired thickness. Drizzle over hot rolls and serve. Frosting keeps well in fridge.

YIELD

Makes 20–25 medium-sized rolls

Cinnamon Bun French Toast

*One Sumptuous Cinnamon Bun makes two pieces of toast.
Figure on three pieces per person.*

Warm the buns in their tin-foil wrapper about 30 minutes in a preheated 300-degree oven until warm. Cut
each bun in two horizontally. Dip each bun in the egg
mixture, coating the cut side generously. Coat only the
one side. Cook on the heated griddle (350 degrees) until the egg is completely cooked.

SERVING SUGGESTIONS

The cinnamon buns are so sweet already that syrup is
too much. Try them plain. If you think they need something, try melted butter with a little jam mixed in.
Raspberry is marvelous.

Sumptuous Cinnamon Buns

1 whisked egg per serving

3 pounds chicken thighs and/or breasts, skin removed

½ cup of your favorite barbecue sauce

¼ cup liquid smoke flavor

½ teaspoon Cajun Jerk or Blackened seasoning

hickory wood chips (optional)

¼ cup chopped onion

¼ cup chopped celery

¼ cup mayonnaise

¼ cup salad dressing

½ teaspoon Dijon-style mustard

8 slices of bread (Italian bread is excellent.)

paprika (optional)

BBQ Chicken Salad Sandwiches

Add a little outdoor flavor to this classic sandwich. This recipe is a great way to use up leftovers from the grill.

Mix barbecue sauce, liquid smoke flavor, and Cajun seasoning. Put chicken in 9-by-13-inch pan and pour sauce on top. Let chicken marinate for an hour, or let it sit overnight in the refrigerator. Start grill and add wood chips to the fire (optional) just before putting chicken on the grill. Put chicken on the grill. Turn after about 15 minutes and cook another 15 minutes. Cook chicken until it is no longer pink in the middle. Cooking times will vary depending on the heat of the fire. Grilling adds the most flavor to the salad, but if you want to bake the chicken instead, preheat the oven to 350 degrees. Cover and bake the chicken for 1 hour. Uncover for the last 10 minutes. Let chicken cool. Take meat off the bone and cut into bite-sized pieces. Add onion, celery, mayonnaise, salad dressing, and mustard and mix well.

Put salad between two slices of bread. Bread can be spread with additional mayonnaise, salad dressing, or mustard. Sandwich can be garnished with lettuce, tomato, and or pickles.

SERVING AND STORAGE SUGGESTIONS

Barbecue chicken salad is also good served over a bed of mixed greens, garnished with tomato and yellow bell pepper. Sprinkle with paprika for a finishing touch of color. Salad needs to be refrigerated. Barbecue chicken can be prepared ahead of time and refrigerated or frozen.

❧ YIELD ❧
Serves 4 generously

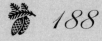

1 cup unsweetened coconut milk

½ cup fresh cilantro, chopped

½ cup brown sugar

⅓ cup green onions

¼ cup soy sauce

4 tablespoons minced garlic

2 tablespoons minced fresh
    ginger

½ teaspoon salt

Coconut Barbecue Sauce

Combine all ingredients in a mixing bowl and blend until smooth. Transfer to a saucepan and heat over medium heat for 5 minutes. Do not boil. Store sauce in refrigerator.

YIELD
Serves 4

Cowboy Coffee Chocolate Layer Cake

Preheat oven to 350 degrees. Grease two 9-inch cake pans per cake. Assemble dry ingredients in mixing bowl and stir. Add wet ingredients and stir until well combined. Pour into pans and bake for 30 minutes. Allow sections to cool at room temperature.

COFFEE SYRUP

Mix water, sugar, and coffee to form a syrup.

FROSTING

Beat all frosting ingredients until creamy. Brush each layer of cake with a couple of tablespoons of coffee syrup, and then frost the cake.

YIELD
Serves 10–12

½ cup cocoa

2 cups flour

1 cup sugar

1 teaspoon instant coffee

1 teaspoon cinnamon

1 cup salad dressing (or 1 cup mayonnaise with 1 tablespoon vinegar)

2 teaspoons baking soda

1 cup cold water

COFFEE SYRUP

6 tablespoons hot water

3 tablespoons sugar

1 tablespoon instant coffee

FROSTING

4 cups powdered sugar

1 stick butter

½ cup cocoa

⅓ cup coffee

4 teaspoons cinnamon

1 teaspoon vanilla

¼ cup milk—if necessary to make it creamy enough to spread

PINE CREEK COOKHOUSE

At an elevation of 8,000 feet, Aspen was no place for Native Americans to spend the winter. But the Ute Indians thrived here during the summertime, hunting and fishing amidst the "Shining Mountains." To the white men who came to the Roaring Fork Valley, the weather was viewed as only a seasonal inconvenience.

Nearby, Leadville had grown to be the second largest city in Colorado by 1879. The discovery of vast quantities of silver and lead had brought many prospectors and miners to Leadville, and they soon crossed the Continental Divide into the Utes' summer hunting territory to discover one of the richest silver lodes the world has ever known.

Their camp was named Ute City at first, but by the following spring the name had been changed to Aspen in recognition of all the evergreen trees covering the hills. While most mining camps were temporary settlements, Aspen developed into a winning combination. Rich silver mines, two very competitive railroads, and money from wealthy businessmen gave Aspen a permanent edge. Jerome B. Wheeler, the former president of Macy's Department Store, and Cincinnati businessman David Hyman are credited with infusing huge sums of money into Aspen and the surrounding mines.

Aspen as a community was so successful that surrounding towns such as Independence, Ashcroft, and Ruby became ghost towns. It wasn't long before the production of silver fields from Aspen's mines had surpassed even rival Leadville, making Aspen the nation's largest single producer.

Economic fortunes changed dramatically in 1893 for all silver-producing communities, and Aspen was hit very hard. The U.S. Government repealed the Sherman Silver Purchase Act that year, taking the nation out of the silver-buying business, and the value of the precious metal plummeted. Only a year later the largest silver nugget ever found, weighing in at 2,200 pounds, was discovered in one of Aspen's mines.

The town had grown to boast 12,000 residents, six newspapers, several schools and banks, electric lights, a modern hospital, theaters, and, like all frontier towns, a brothel district. Even as residents departed for better opportunities, the town hung on as a rural county seat and ranching center.

By 1935 just 700 people were left in Aspen; then, new wealth was discovered in the area's abundance of white powdery snow. International outdoorsmen came to the Roaring Fork Valley to establish a ski resort. Their first efforts were focused on the nearby ghost town of Ashcroft, but they canceled their plans when WWII broke out. An alternative plan resulted in ski run on nearby Aspen Mountain.

The war actually brought the Army's 10th Mountain Division to the area; they received training at nearby Camp Hale. Many soldiers took leave to ski in Aspen, among them Austrian Friedl Pfeifer. After the war, Pfeifer teamed up with Chicago industrialist Walter Paepcke and his wife, who were interested in the community's potential as a summertime cultural center. Pfeifer wanted to build a ski resort to compete with Europe's best.

In 1947 Aspen boasted of the world's longest ski lift. In 1949, Paepcke, with the University of Chicago, masterminded the Goethe Bicentennial Convocation in Aspen. The town celebrated the great humanist's 200th birthday with international leaders, artists, and musicians. The music, art, dance, theater, and international studies programs that developed assured Aspen's role as a cultural center. In 1950, Aspen became the first ski resort in America to host an international competition, a precursor of today's World Cup races.

The Pine Creek Cookhouse is located on a hill just outside the ghost town of Ashcroft. Every meal is greatly enhanced by the abundance of stunning mountain scenery that surrounds this mountain retreat.

Pine Creek Cookhouse
314 South 2nd Street
Aspen, Colorado 81611
(970) 925-1044

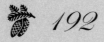
5 garlic cloves

2 whole shallots

¾ cup maple syrup

1 cup balsamic vinegar

¼ cup Dijon mustard

2 cups salad oil

salt and pepper

3 eggs

2 anchovies

2 tablespoons Dijon mustard

2 tablespoons chopped garlic

⅛ cup lemon juice

½ ounce sherry vinegar

1 tablespoon Worcestershire
  sauce

1 teaspoon Tabasco sauce

⅓ cup grated Parmesan cheese

⅓ tablespoon kosher salt

⅛ teaspoon black pepper

2 cups salad oil

½ to 1 cup water

Cookhouse Dressing

Combine first 5 ingredients in blender and mix until smooth. Slowly add 2 cups salad oil. Blend. Add salt and pepper to taste.

Caesar Dressing

Combine all ingredients except salad oil and water in blender or food processor, and puree to the max. Slowly add 2 cups of salad oil. Add ½ to 1 cup water to thin.

Chocolate Decadence

In a double boiler, melt chocolate and butter until completely melted. In a mixer add eggs and sugar by beating with a paddle on high. Add water. When frothy foam forms on egg mixture, remove from mixer and *slowly* fold into chocolate mix in an 8-inch square pan. Bake at 375 degrees for 1 to 1½ hours, or a toothpick comes out clean.

DECADENCE ICING
Combine ingredients in a saucepan and occasionally stir until well melted and liquid. Frost the decadence.

18 ounces chocolate

¾ cup butter

6 eggs

¾ cup sugar

1 cup water

DECADENCE ICING

½ cup corn syrup

½ cup cream

9 ounces chocolate

RAPIDS LODGE

Grand Lake has attracted people for hundreds of years. Fish and wild game, vast stands of virgin timber, precious minerals, and breathtaking vistas have all drawn man to the area. The Ute, Arapaho, Sioux, and Cheyenne Indians all ventured to the Grand Lake region in search of wild game, which both fed and clothed their families. The Native Americans fought with each other over control of the area, but it was the white man who would dominate it completely.

European trappers searched for beaver pelts in the Rocky Mountains, and later explorers arrived searching for the headwaters of the "Grand River," renamed the Colorado River in 1921. Beginning at Grand Lake, the mighty Colorado River flows through Lake Granby, Grand Junction, Grand Mesa, past Moab, Utah, and into Canyonlands National Park in Utah. The river is best known as the instrument of nature that carved out the Grand Canyon.

When the Colorado gold rush of 1859 attracted prospectors to the Grand Lake area, access remained limited to foot trails. As wagon roads followed the miners, the community experienced rapid growth, and Grand Lake began attracting a variety of settlers. They were not idle. In 1875 silver, lead, copper, and gold ore were discovered in the Never Summer Range.

The town of Grand Lake was surveyed in 1881, the same year that 18-year-old John Lapsley Ish arrived in town. "Laps" Ish had been 3 months old when his father took his family from Missouri in a covered wagon; he was 6 months old when they reached Denver in 1863. While his father pursued farming, Laps came to Grand Lake to mine. After 4 years he became a mail carrier—a particularly arduous position during the harsh winters.

Laps eventually married and homesteaded near Rand. Not having succeeded at mining, he saw the value of offering services to the miners and built the Rand Hotel, which he operated with his wife until 1910. After a brief move to California, the family came back to Granby, opening the Middle Park Auto Company garage. He then ran a stage line to Grand Lake.

Returning to the hotel business, Laps built the Rapids Lodge in 1915, using the plentiful lodgepole pines in the area. Being particularly industrious, Ish had built a sawmill on the site to provide himself and others with lumber. The lodge had running water and baths, with electricity provided by an "overshot" water wheel in the nearby Tonahutu River.

The Ish family operated the Rapids Lodge in Grand Lake for many years. The Pine Cone Inn was also built by Ish and managed by his son. Part of the Rapids Lodge was built using the original packing boxes Ish used to ship his belongings to Grand Lake. One of these boxes with Ish's name printed on it is still visible in a storage room in the restaurant.

Ish died in 1943, and the lodge has passed to approximately 30 owners. In the 1950s the second floor of the historic building was a casino and the third floor was a brothel. Management employed an emergency buzzer under the front desk, so that people upstairs could be alerted when the law stopped in. Staff and guests could exit the building via the back doors. During the 1960s Jim Croce, Kris Kristofferson, and Janis Joplin all played at the Rapids when the restaurant area was a thriving honky-tonk.

People who believe in ghosts say there is a friendly old lady who wanders the corridors, moves and hides items, and opens and closes doors. She used to drink a bit, and one day her husband just disappeared and was never found. Some say they have seen him too. When you visit the Rapids Lodge, you will see a piece of Colorado history.

Rapids Lodge and Restaurant
209 Rapids Lane
PO Box 1400
Grand Lake, Colorado 80447
(970) 627-3707

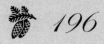
Pomegranate Splash

Fill rocks glass with ice. Pour 4 ounces of vodka over ice. Add a splash of Pama. Garnish with a lime twist.

4 ounces "Pearl" pomegranate vodka

"Pama" pomegranate liqueur

Maple Balsamic Vinaigrette

Whisk first four ingredients in a small bowl until blended, then add shallot. Store in refrigerator.

2 tablespoons olive oil, extra virgin

2 tablespoons balsamic vinegar

2 tablespoons maple syrup

2 teaspoons Dijon mustard

1 shallot, finely diced

salt and pepper to taste

Shitake Seared Alaskan Halibut

As featured in Bon Appetit *magazine*

Melt 2 tablespoons of butter in heavy, medium skillet over medium heat. Add shallots and sauté until soft (about 2 minutes). Add wine and cook until most of the wine evaporates (about 2 minutes). Add cream and simmer until sauce thickens slightly.

Cut 4 tablespoons of butter into ½-inch cubes and add to sauce, a few cubes at a time, whisking until incorporated before adding more. Whisk in lemon juice and season with salt and pepper. Remove from heat. Cover the beurre blanc to keep it warm while cooking the fish.

Preheat oven to 350 degrees.

Place mushrooms in a blender and grind to a fine powder. Transfer the powder to a plate and sprinkle fillets with salt and pepper. Press fillets into mushroom powder to coat on both sides. Melt the remaining 4 tablespoons of butter in a large ovenproof skillet over medium-high heat, and add fillets to skillet. Sauté until golden brown on bottom (about 3 minutes).

Turn over and transfer to oven; bake until opaque in center (about 7 minutes).

Place fillets on four plates. Drizzle with beurre blanc and serve. Bon Appetit!

BEURRE BLANC

10 tablespoons chilled butter

½ cup chopped shallots

¼ cup dry white wine

¾ cup whipping cream

2 teaspoons fresh lemon juice

½-ounce package dried shitake mushrooms

four 6-ounce halibut fillets

YIELD

Serves 4

REDSTONE INN

First there was gold, then there was silver, and they both brought hordes of people to Colorado seeking their fortunes. Along the way, the miners and prospectors also discovered coal. One of the industrialists who came to Colorado to pursue the coal business was John Cleveland Osgood, a cousin of President Grover Cleveland. Anticipating that coal would be an industry in itself, Osgood founded the Colorado Fuel and Iron Company in Crystal River Valley.

As his business expanded, Osgood felt it was not only necessary to take care of his employees in order to keep them, but it was also the right thing to do. He constructed 84 cottages to house his coal workers who had families, and he erected a 20-room inn just for his bachelor employees. The facilities featured indoor plumbing and electricity, which were unusual luxuries back then. Modern bathhouse facilities, a clubhouse with a library and a theater, and a school were also provided for the "cokers" and their families.

Thus was born the community of Redstone, located in the Elk Mountain area of southwest Pitkin County approximately 16 miles south of Carbondale. Many of these Craftsman-era, Swiss-style cottages are still in use today.

Referred to as "the Ruby of the Rockies," Redstone was developed entirely as a company town. And it was the success of the coal business that kept the town going. The high-grade coking coal of the Coal Basin area, 4½ miles west of Redstone, was like gold to the town. The cokers worked in Redstone's beehive coking ovens, which were used to transform raw coal into the high-grade coke used in the production of steel.

Osgood's coal empire brought much more than houses to Redstone. The development of the coal business also spurred the construction of the Crystal River Railroad. This rail line connected the coal mines up-valley to the main lines in Carbondale, and the coke was then transported to the steel mills in Pueblo. By 1900 the mining operations at Coal Basin and Redstone were in full swing. Between 1900 and 1909, 249 coking ovens produced 11,000 tons of high-grade coke a month for the Pueblo steel mill.

But it was Osgood's second wife, Alma, who made the greatest impression on Redstone's early 20th-century inhabitants. Thought to have been a Swedish countess before coming to the United States, and possessed of a great sense of obligation, Alma became known as "Lady Bountiful" for the generosity she showed toward the coal workers and their families.

And it was for his Alma that Osgood constructed "Cleveholm Manor," the opulent 42-room Tudor-style mansion now commonly referred to as "the Redstone Castle." By the time Cleveholm was completed in 1902, the estate included servants' quarters, a gamekeeper's lodge, a carriage house, and a greenhouse. Alma hosted lavish parties at Cleveholm. Dinner was followed by music for the ladies, while the men played billiards in the game room.

In 1903 Osgood, who was considered to be one of the nation's five wealthiest individuals at the time, lost control of his company. It passed to John D. Rockefeller and George Gould, who purchased the public stock. He kept ownership of the town, however, and Redstone continued to house workers. In 1909 the mine and coking camp were closed down. Osgood disappeared from public view; but in 1925, he returned to Cleveholm with his third wife, Lucille. He oversaw considerable renovation of the manor as well as the employee quarters before he died a year later.

The elegant inn built for the bachelor employees is now the Redstone Inn. It is an integral part of Redstone's history as well as the remainder of the mining operations. Today 44 of the coke ovens survive across the river, along with about 20 cottages and small buildings along Redstone Boulevard.

Redstone Inn
82 Redstone Boulevard
Redstone, Colorado 81623
(800) 748-2524
(970) 963-2526

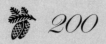

1 pound unsalted butter

1 cup sugar

1 tablespoon vanilla extract

berries of your choice (we use
  a mix of blueberries and
  strawberries)

1 cup Chambord or raspberry
  liqueur

1 cup rum

vanilla ice cream

blackberries for garnish

mint sprig for garnish

Berries Chambord

Soften the butter, then mix in the vanilla and sugar. Cut the berries into halves or quarters, depending on type of berries used. You may use frozen berries since they will be cooked.

Combine the rum and berry liqueur.

Note: Do not attempt to prepare more than four servings at one time; the flames from the flambé may get out of hand.

TO PREPARE TWO SERVINGS

In a 9- or 10-inch sauté pan, place approximately 2–3 strawberries and ¼ cup blueberries per serving cup of the butter-sugar mixture. Place pan on high heat. When butter is almost completely melted, add about 2 cups of your berry mixture. Bring the berries to a simmer and add approximately 2 ounces of the liquor. If you are cooking with gas, tilt the edge of the pan toward the flame and the alcohol should ignite. If cooking with on an electric stove, you may use a match—or better yet, an extended lighter made for lighting grills or fireplaces.

Lightly agitate the berries using wrist action until all alcohol is burned off. When the alcohol has burned off, the berries are ready to serve.

In a large shallow bowl, place two or three scoops of vanilla ice cream. Pour the berries around the ice cream. Serve with a biscotto.

Signature Tortilla Soup

Marinate the chicken breasts in olive oil and soy sauce.

Combine onions, celery, red peppers, green chilies, and spices with oil in a large, heavy-bottomed pot. Sauté over medium heat until onions are translucent.

Add the next four ingredients. Do *not* drain tomatoes. Bring to a simmer, stirring often to avoid scorching. Simmer and stir for 20 minutes uncovered to reduce. Salt to taste.

Fifteen minutes before service, add tomatillos. Grill the chicken breasts. When grilled, julienne the chicken. Five minutes before service, add the corn.

Serve in large soup plates. Garnish each bowl with clusters of freshly grilled, julienned chicken breasts (½ breast per serving), ¼ of an avocado fanned into slices, cilantro sprigs, and tortilla chips.

YIELD

Serves 8

4 chicken breasts

⅛ cup olive oil

½ teaspoon soy sauce

2 cups yellow onions, diced ¼ inch

½ cup celery, diced ¼ inch

¼ cup roasted red pepper, diced ¼ inch

¼ cup green chilies, canned, diced

1 teaspoon ground coriander

1½ tablespoon dark chili powder

½ tablespoon ground black pepper

½ large garlic cloves, peeled and sliced

⅛ cup chopped cilantro

2 cups canned tomatoes, diced

2 cups black beans, canned

2 cups pinto beans

6 cups chicken stock

½ cup fresh tomatillos, quartered

½ cup cut corn, fresh or frozen

¼ avocado per serving

cilantro sprigs

tortilla chips (yellow or blue corn)

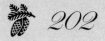

3 pounds Yukon gold potatoes, peeled and diced to 1 inch (approximately 2 quarts)

3 quarts water

¼ cup cleaned and coarsely chopped leeks

½ cup (packed) coarsely chopped scallion greens

½ cup milk

½ cup heavy cream

¼ pound butter

½ teaspoon white pepper

2 teaspoons salt

Scallion Mashed Potatoes

The fun spring-green color of scallion mashed potatoes adds zest to any dinner!

Place potatoes in lightly salted water and bring to a low boil until tender.

Place leeks, scallions, and milk in a bar blender and blend until a uniform green color (about 1 minute).

Combine cream, milk and scallion mixture, butter, white pepper, and salt in a saucepan and bring to a simmer. Drain potatoes and run through a grinder with the smallest plate (or a food mill).

Place ground potatoes and hot cream into a mixing bowl. With the whip attachment, mix on medium for about 30 seconds, then scrape the sides of the bowl and mix for another 30 seconds. (Potatoes should be a uniformly green color.) Do not overmix, or potatoes will get starchy.

Reheat for service, or cool for storage. Potatoes may be frozen in Ziploc bags in meal-sized portions to be reheated in microwave.

Southwest

NEW SHERIDAN HOTEL

The Ute Indians figured it out centuries ago. They spent their summer and fall by the San Miguel River, hunting and fishing. When the winter arrived they headed for the desert canyons that provided some relief from the weather. When Spanish explorers arrived in the 1700s, they named the San Juan Mountains in honor of a saint.

But it was gold and the white prospectors invading the San Juans and the San Miguel Valley that made it prosper. The mountains also contained zinc, lead, copper, iron, and silver, all attracting additional settlers from the East. Thus began a mining boom that flooded the valley with humanity.

The camp at the head of the San Miguel River grew slowly beginning in 1875. In 1879 prospectors were washing the gold dust from the gravel deposits above the riverbed. There was some gold dust to be found in the gravel, but it was the silver discovered high on the steep mountain slopes above the upper San Miguel River Valley that accelerated the growth of the community.

When Telluride was founded in 1880, it was originally called Columbia. This name eventually raised a conflict with the town of Columbia, California. The people in Colorado needed their own post office, so the name was changed to Telluride in anticipation of great things to come. *Telluride* is derived from tellurium, a mineral associated with gold, but was never actually found in the San Juans.

The lure of gold brought more people, and more people brought the railroads. They were a major part of the development of the area. Not only could people come and go more easily, but the wealth of all the mountains could be more easily converted to good living. Colorado Avenue, also called Main Street, offered stores of all kinds, lodging, and the post office. Telluride also had many saloons and bordellos, many of which are still standing today.

In 1889 Robert Leroy Parker, better known as Butch Cassidy, and Harry Longbaugh, "The Sundance Kid," came to Telluride with their gang. The Wild Bunch robbed the San Miguel County Bank, making off with $24,000 of the miners' monthly payroll. The bank's owner and a posse went after them, but the money was never recovered.

In 1891 a three-story wooden frame structure called the Sheridan Hotel was opened. Just like the town itself, the hotel was built in the distinguished Victorian style, a reflection of the riches of the gold and silver strikes in the surrounding San Juan Mountains. Like the transitory wealth of some of the miners, the wooden hotel didn't last long. Three years later, in 1894, the original building was destroyed by fire. Undaunted, the owners rebuilt the hotel next door, this time out of brick. The New Sheridan Hotel opened in 1895 and has been welcoming guests for over 100 years.

An extensive renovation in 1995 returned this historic property to its former glory and included the renowned New Sheridan Chop House and additional rooms. But the décor of the New Sheridan Bar has been virtually unchanged since it opened in 1895. It is a unique opportunity to take a trip back in time. The New Sheridan Hotel is dedicated to faithfully maintaining the historic integrity, architecture, and ambience of the original hotel.

New Sheridan Hotel
231 West Colorado Avenue (Main Street)
Telluride, Colorado 81435
(970) 728-9100

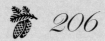

RAGOUT

5 cups chanterelle mushrooms

5 cups portobello mushrooms

5 cups shitake mushrooms

5 cups morel mushrooms

5 cups oyster mushrooms

four 6-ounce short loins
    or tenderloins of elk

1 tablespoon chopped garlic

1 tablespoon chopped shallots

2 tablespoons chopped sage

1 cup red wine

1½ cups demi-glace (veal stock)

salt and pepper to taste

2 tablespoons butter

Elk with Roasted Wild Mushroom Ragout

Slice all mushrooms and toss lightly with oil, salt, and pepper. Roast in 350-degree oven until lightly browned.

Grill elk until rare. In a hot saucepan, add mushrooms, garlic, sage, and shallots to a little butter. Deglaze with red wine and reduce by half. Add veal stock and reduce by half. Add salt and pepper and finish with cold butter. Slice elk, and top with slightly saucy ragout.

YIELD

Serves 4

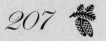

Crab Cakes with Jalapeno-Mint Aioli

CRAB CAKES

Combine all ingredients and shape into cakes. Pan-fry in clarified butter.

AIOLI

In a food processor, combine all ingredients except for oil. Blend until slightly emulsified. Very slowly add oil to mix while machine is running. Check to make sure seasoning is correct.

"If there is food in the house, a guest is no worry."

—Pashto proverb

CRAB CAKES

1 pound backfin crabmeat

2 eggs

⅔ cup Japanese bread crumbs

1 tablespoon chopped fresh parsley

1 pinch cayenne pepper

1 pinch salt

juice of 1 lemon, freshly squeezed

AIOLI

4 egg yolks

1 clove garlic

juice of 1 lemon

1 tablespoon jalapeno powder

1 tablespoon salt

1 cup chopped fresh mint

1½ cups canola and olive oil blend

POWDERHORN GUEST RANCH

The Powderhorn Valley sits high up on the Colorado Plateau. Nestled in Gunnison County, it has a rich and varied history. The area was home to the Ute and Paiute Indian tribes for thousands of years, before Mexican explorers and, later, beaver trappers came to the valley. In the early 1800s beaver pelts along with other animal hides were major industries in the United States.

The 1840s brought prospectors searching for gold, but it was not until 1858–59 that gold was discovered near what is now Denver. It wasn't long before swarms of people descended on Colorado in search of their fortunes. The Powderhorn Valley became the center of the Gunnison Gold Belt, a 300-square-mile area that produced good quantities of gold from a number of mines. Later, deposits of silver and coal—and more recently, molybdenum—were discovered and have continued to excite miners and prospectors.

The Atchison, Topeka, and Santa Fe Railway and the Denver and Rio Grande Railroad were a major boost to the valley's economy from the 1860 until the 1890s. Trains meant not only that more miners and prospectors could come in but also that ore could be shipped out quickly to major population centers.

The railroad was also an incentive for the stagecoach industry. Stagecoaches created some of the routes that the railroads eventually used, but they also went places the railroad did not go. And many railroad stations had stage service to the small towns that otherwise were isolated. The Powderhorn Valley was home to the Barlow-Sanderson Stage, which ran from Enid, Oklahoma, through Powderhorn and on to Sacramento, California.

The Powderhorn Valley saw many famous names. Captain John Gunnison mapped the area, earning the distinction of having the county named after him. The great military explorer John C. Fremont came through this area, searching for an easy route to the West. Doc Holliday and Wyatt and Virgil Earp stayed in the area for some time, mostly involved in gambling but also investing in mines.

In the late 1890s the Powderhorn Ranch began. It was then called "the Thompson Place," after Will and Violet Thompson, who had come to Colorado from Oklahoma. Will had been a "shotgun" rider for the stagecoach, and he frequently wrote his wife about the Powderhorn Valley. When Will had saved up enough money, he moved his wife west, and they opened the Thompson Place as a stage stop on the Barlow-Sanderson route. The Thompsons ran it as a guest ranch where stagecoach passengers could get a cabin, a bath, a hot meal, and dance in the Ross Lodge. They could also try their hand at gold panning or horse riding.

In the 1930s, a frequent guest and automotive pioneer and inventor bought the ranch and changed the name to the Six J's, one J for each of the first names of his daughters. Later, the inventor of the pogo stick, Ralph Frantz, ran the property as a dude and guest ranch with his wife, Hazel, and their daughters until the 1970s. Jim and Bonnie Cook bought the ranch in the 1970s and changed the name to the Powderhorn Ranch in honor of the surrounding valley. Greg and Shelly Williams bought Powderhorn Guest Ranch in 1999 and have operated it since then.

Powderhorn Ranch is surrounded by 1.4 million acres of national forest and government land, and it backs up to over 64,000 acres of the Powderhorn Primitive Wilderness. The management is dedicated to providing an authentic Western dude ranch experience in a beautiful Rocky Mountain setting.

Powderhorn Guest Ranch
1525 County Road 27
Powderhorn, Colorado 81243
(800) 786-1220

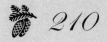

Powderhorn Chocolate Torte Cake

1 cup unsalted butter

8 ounces semisweet chocolate, chopped

5 large eggs

¼ cup sugar

⅓ cup dark corn syrup

GLAZE

¾ cup whipping cream

8 ounces semisweet chocolate, chopped

1½ tablespoons unsalted butter, room temperature

1½ tablespoons light corn syrup

Preheat oven to 350 degrees. Butter and flour a 9-inch diameter cake pan with 2-inch sides. Line the bottom of pan with parchment. Dust the pan with flour and tap out excess.

Stir butter and chocolate in heavy medium saucepan over low heat until smooth.

Set aside.

Using an electric mixer, beat eggs and sugar in a large bowl until slightly thickened.

Add corn syrup and beat until slowly dissolving ribbons form when beaters are lifted. Pour chocolate mixture into the egg mixture and fold together gently. Pour batter into prepared pan. Bake until tip of knife inserted into center comes out clean, about 1 hour.

Cool completely in pan on rack.

Invert cake onto 7½-inch cardboard round. Peel off parchment. Place cake on cardboard on a rack set over a cookie sheet.

GLAZE

Bring cream to simmer in a heavy medium saucepan. Reduce heat to low.

Add chocolate and stir until melted. Remove from heat and let it stand until just cool.

Whisk in butter and syrup. Pour glaze over cake. Spread with spatula to cover top and sides. Refrigerate cake overnight. (This dessert can be prepared up to three days ahead. Cover and keep refrigerated.) Cut cake into slices. Serve cold.

Note: I always use Ghirardelli or Godiva chocolate for the glaze—or instead of a glaze, you can melt any chocolate and use plastic gloves to drizzle it decoratively by hand over the torte. I also make my whipping cream (heavy whipping cream with a teaspoon of extract—peppermint, almond, etc., or Amaretto liqueur).

Egg Bake with San Juan Salsa

6 slices of bread, cubed

4 eggs

2 cups of milk

1 teaspoon dried mustard

12 ounces shredded cheddar
cheese

1 pound breakfast sausage,
browned

SALSA

10 Roma tomatoes, diced

2 jalapenos, diced

½ cup diced onion

3 cups diced melon
(peach, mango,
or a fruit you prefer)

½ cup blueberries

salt to taste

Whip the eggs, milk, and dry mustard together. In a 9-by-13-inch pan, layer the bread, sausage, and cheddar cheese in that order. Pour the milk and egg mixture over the top. Bake at 325 degrees for 1 hour.

SALSA

Mix all ingredients 24 hours before serving, for optimum flavor.

YIELD

Serves 8

STRATER HOTEL

Silver and gold built the city of Durango. Nestled in the midst of some of the world's most beautiful mountain scenery, Durango has an exceptionally colorful history. Miners by the scores began to flock to the area in the 1870s to seek their fortune after word got out that gold had been discovered. The town of Durango was conceived by the Denver and Rio Grande Western Railroad Company, established in 1879. Company officials planned and laid out the beautiful and historic downtown that remains today, although it started out much differently. When the railroad first arrived in August of 1881, Durango was referred to as the new "City in the Wilderness," or "Smelter City," because it was host to the region's growing smelting, mining, and agricultural economy.

With the new rail transportation and the quick money made by the numerous area miners, it wasn't long before enterprising merchants, saloon gals, ranchers, and farmers settled into the valley, lending a balance to the city's economy and culture. These newcomers built churches, schools, and many of the fine buildings and Victorian homes still standing today.

Durango was intended to be the most modern city in Colorado. Nothing could compare to it, if the railroad company had anything to say about it. Progress appeared in the late 1880s and early 1890s, in the form of a grand hotel (the four-story brick Strater), electric lights with a home-owned electric company, the telephone, an electric trolley, and a three-story building with an electric elevator (the Newman Building at 800 Main).

The rapidly growing business district along Main Avenue and grand homes on the 3rd Avenue Boulevard helped Durango fulfill its self-proclaimed destiny as the business capital of the region. Its brilliant future as a residential and business center for the Four Corners region (Arizona, New Mexico, Utah, and Colorado) became ever more secure.

The area's rich history actually predates the development of Durango by at least 1,300 years. The mild climate, fertile soils, and abundant wild game first attracted the ancestral Puebloan culture in around AD 700. At one time in Colorado's ancient history, the area's human population was actually larger than it is today. Some of the most spectacular and well-preserved Puebloan ruins in the United States are found within a 100-mile radius of the Strater Hotel. The most famous site is Mesa Verde National Park. Also nearby are the Aztec Ruins, Chaco Canyon, and the Salmon Ruins that display the ancestral Puebloan culture in its various stages of development and decline.

As Durango's future was being shaped, a very young Cleveland pharmacist named Henry Strater decided that Durango would need a grand hotel. Strater had the nerve and drive to build it, but he also had three significant handicaps. He lacked the money necessary, he had no experience in the hotel business, and he was still a minor and legally could not enter into a contract. Undeterred, he fibbed a bit about his age, borrowed money, and plowed ahead. Construction was a challenge; but with the help of his two brothers and a lot of enthusiasm, Henry's dream was realized. The Strater Hotel finally opened—after an expenditure of $70,000 and placement of 376,000 native red bricks and hand-carved sandstone cornices and sills.

As it evolved, the Strater proved to be a popular winter retreat with travelers and locals alike. Some Durango residents closed their own homes during the cold winter months and moved into the hotel. Each room boasted its own wood-burning stove and comfortable furniture, and a few rooms were equipped with pianos and washstands. The washstands served double duty, for the cabinet also housed a makeshift water closet that was emptied each morning by the maids. The hotel also boasted a unique three-story privy, with very strategically placed holes.

Henry Strater chose to run his pharmacy from the prominent corner of the hotel, leasing the rooming operation to H. L. Rice. Under Rice's management, the Strater soon became the town's primary place of social gathering. Women convened in the winter to play euchre, while Rice entertained their children. Rice was known for having a warm heart for children, although he was a stern businessman.

Being young and inexperienced, Strater quickly discovered that he had neglected to exclude his pharmacy location in the lease to Rice. Rice extracted an extremely large rent, which infuriated the young pharmacist and prompted him in 1893 to build the competing Columbian Hotel directly to the south, with the intent of putting Rice out of business. Both hotels competed toe to toe until 1895, when the silver panic put both properties out of business.

The Bank of Cleveland repossessed the Strater and sold it to Ms. Hattie Mashburn and Charles E. Stilwell. Both had enough hotel experience to make things work in the toughest of times. Stilwell took the hotel through the turn of the century and developed a rather more refined appeal through such offerings as opera and fine dinners.

Durango's economy got a boost when oil and gas were discovered in the area. In 1926, a group of Durango businessmen formed an organization to buy the now aging hotel, and the group focused on refreshing its image. Although the townsfolk no longer withdraw to the Strater in winter months, a few noted personages have made the Strater their home away from home. Western author Louis L'Amour always asked for room 222, directly above the Diamond Belle Saloon. He said the honky-tonk music helped set the mood for his novels of the Old West. A good portion of his Sackett novels were written at the Strater.

Built in 1887 without "modern conveniences," the Strater has enjoyed ongoing renovation. The journey into creating the Victorian charm in the décor began on a trip to a hotel convention in Atlanta, Georgia, where new owners Earl and Jentra Barker found an authentic Victorian bed in an antique store. They decided it would be interesting to furnish several of the larger rooms with authentic period furniture, and they cashed in their airline tickets and drove back to Durango pulling a trailer, stopping at antique stores along the way. This unusual beginning of the hotel's collection of American Victorian-era walnut furniture has grown into the largest assemblage of its kind in the world today.

Strater Hotel
699 Main Avenue
Durango, Colorado 81301
(970) 247-4431

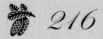
four 5- or 6-ounce portions elk
   tenderloin with silver skin
   removed

BLACKBERRY-SAGE SAUCE

1 tablespoon olive oil

2 shallots, fine diced

1 cup blackberries,
   fresh or frozen

2 cups beef stock

¼ cup Madeira wine

3 tablespoons sugar

2 tablespoons chopped fresh sage
   (about 2 sprigs)

salt and black pepper to taste

3 ounces heavy cream

½ teaspoon cornstarch
   for thickening

Charbroiled Elk Tenderloin
with Blackberry-Sage Sauce

Cook the elk until medium rare and no more. Due to
the leanness of the meat, elk tends to be tough and dry
if overcooked.

BLACKBERRY-SAGE SAUCE

In a medium saucepan over medium high heat, add the
olive oil and shallots and cook for 2–3 minutes. Add the
blackberries, sugar, and sage and cook for about 5 minutes more.

Deglaze the pan with the Madeira wine, stir in completely, and then add the beef stock. Bring to a boil,
then reduce to a hard simmer and let it cook for 8–10
minutes to let the flavors combine.

Thicken the sauce to a fluid consistency with the cornstarch as needed, let it cook for 3 minutes more, and
then add heavy cream. Mix the cream in thoroughly
and adjust the flavor with salt and pepper. Remove
from heat and let the sauce cool, then blend in a
blender until smooth. Bring the sauce back to temperature and enjoy.

YIELD

Serves 4

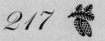

Coconut-Pretzel-Crusted Shrimp
with Rum-Dijon Sauce

Mix together chopped pretzels, coconut, and bread crumbs in a bowl and set aside. Combine the eggs and the water in a separate container for the egg wash. In another bowl, combine flour with salt and pepper.

Toss shrimp with the flour mixture until well coated. Then place them in the egg wash, where they will sit for 1–2 minutes so that the egg wash will penetrate the flour coating. Remove the shrimp from the egg wash and let it drain in a colander for about 2 minutes. Then, one at a time, put the shrimp into the coconut-pretzel mixture, pressing the coating into the shrimp. Set the coated shrimp on a cookie sheet.

Shrimp can be either deep- or pan-fried until golden brown, about 3–4 minutes.

RUM-DIJON SAUCE
Put all ingredients into a bowl, whisk together, and it's ready to serve. Enjoy.

Note: This sauce is served cold and can be made up to 1 week in advance.

12 uncooked jumbo shrimp, peeled, deveined, and butterflied

1 cup coarsely chopped pretzels

1 cup coconut

1 cup panko bread crumbs (Japanese bread crumbs)

3 whole eggs

½ cup water

1 cup seasoned flour

RUM-DIJON SAUCE

3 ounces Malibu rum

2 ounces coconut extract

3 ounces rice vinegar

1 cup Dijon mustard

1 tablespoon sugar

1 tablespoon honey

salt and pepper to taste

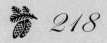

½ head Romaine lettuce

½ head green leaf lettuce

3 cups baby greens mix

1 pinch salt

Rustin's Raspberry Vinaigrette
(recipe follows)

SALAD TOPPINGS

1½ cups red grapes, cut in half

garlic crostini (recipe follows)

1 tomato, small and diced

1 tablespoon chopped parsley

½ cup toasted walnuts

6 ounces Gorgonzola cheese

GARLIC CROSTINI

8–10 slices French bread

2 tablespoons garlic

¼ cup olive oil

2 tablespoons Parmesan cheese

1 tablespoon parsley

salt and pepper to taste

1 tablespoon chopped basil

Gorgonzola Salad
with Rustin's Raspberry Vinaigrette

Cut head lettuces into 1-inch cubes, then wash and dry thoroughly. In large chilled metal bowl, toss the three types of greens, add a pinch of salt, and toss with raspberry vinaigrette just before serving.

SALAD TOPPINGS

Scatter grape halves, toasted walnuts, and Gorgonzola cheese over the top of salad. Scatter edge of serving plate with parsley and diced tomato. Top salad with two pieces of crisp garlic crostini.

GARLIC CROSTINI

Preheat oven to 325–350 degrees. Slice baguette on bias, then smear bottom of cookie sheet with olive oil, just enough to coat. Mix remaining olive oil and garlic together. Arrange cut bread on pan and spoon mixed oil on top of bread slices. Season with parsley, basil, salt, pepper, and Parmesan cheese. Bake in preheated oven until crisp.

RUSTIN'S RASPBERRY VINAIGRETTE (MAKES 1 QUART)

In a large mixing bowl, place chopped raspberries and onions. Add vinegar, seasonings, and sugar. Let the mixture marinate for 10 minutes. While constantly whisking, add oil and water. Check for flavor and adjust as needed. Chill at least 2 hours.

To serve, strain chilled dressing and pour over mixed field greens with red halved grapes, toasted walnuts, and crumbled Gorgonzola cheese.

RUSTIN'S RASPBERRY VINAIGRETTE (MAKES 1 QUART)

3 cups fresh chopped raspberries (frozen raspberries may be substituted)

¾ cup raspberry wine vinegar

¾ cup basil

½ teaspoon oregano

1½ teaspoons granulated garlic

⅓ cup fine-diced red onion

1½ teaspoons salt

¾ teaspoon white pepper

½ cup sugar

1 dash Worcestershire sauce

3 cups olive oil

½ cup water

WAUNITA HOT SPRINGS RANCH

Waunita Hot Springs was originally home to the Moache band of the Ute Indians who hunted and fished in the area for centuries. Legend says that the Spanish came to the area because the French had already found gold here. The conquistadores had already explored the area, and the Spanish government had claimed the territory for itself; but Napoleon Bonaparte believed there were significant amounts of gold to be had.

Needing money to finance his military ambitions, Napoleon had a group of Frenchmen organized in New Orleans to search for the gold, hoping to find and retrieve it before the land was sold. The legend says that the French found a lot of gold, which they turned into ingots before most of them perished from exposure to the mercury used in the process. They also found the Indians who were employed by the Spanish to wipe them out.

Napoleon sold the Louisiana Purchase in 1803 for $15 million, before any gold was returned to France. What became of the gold the French found is unclear. Two cowboys were lost in the mountains during a snowstorm in 1878, and they took shelter in a small cave. Inside they discovered a cache of gold bars, believed to be from the French mining adventure decades earlier. After reaching civilization with a bar of gold each, they attempted to retrace their steps—but they never found the cave again. The story has consumed many fortune seekers since then, but no one has ever found this cache of gold bars, if indeed it ever existed.

The gold rush of 1859 rapidly changed the nature of the area. When gold was discovered in Colorado, people came from the East as well as from the West to find riches in the Colorado Mountains along the Continental Divide. What was left of the Ute Indian tribes was driven out of the area by the white settlers. Camps became towns, and some towns became cities.

The oldest records show that the first resident of the springs was Colonel Robert Moore in 1879. He had a hotel built in 1885, but he eventually sold his interests to a doctor from Chicago. Dr. Charles Gilbert Davis is credited with changing the name from Tomichi Hot Springs, as it was originally known, to Waunita Hot Springs.

The town of Waunita Hot Springs was homesteaded in the 1880s following the discovery of silver. Always supportive of miners and prospectors working the area hills, Waunita Hot Springs really became famous for the hot springs, which disgorged approximately 300,000 gallons per day of 170-degree water. Dr. Davis brought his patients out to spend the summers and bathe in the healing waters. For anyone who wasn't his patient, he advised that they drink at least four glasses of Waunita spring water each day.

The repeal of the Sherman Silver Purchase Act in 1893 dealt a terrific blow to Colorado's economy, and Waunita Hot Springs suffered too. When in 1903 gold was discovered in Bowerman, 5 miles upstream from Waunita, the area got another short-lived economic boost. What kept the area going was Dr. Davis's claim of the healing properties of the hot springs.

After Davis died in 1928, the Depression caused a series of owners to operate the facility. The doctor's daughter and her second husband began operating the property as a guest ranch. This idea was greatly improved upon by the Pringles, who have owned the property since 1962.

Waunita Hot Springs Ranch is located high in the Colorado Rockies, at an elevation of 8,946 feet. It is 10 miles west of the Continental Divide, surrounded by Gunnison National Forest land and summer pasture. U.S. Forest Service permits and private leases enable guests to enjoy the use of hundreds of thousands of acres in eastern Gunnison County. The ranch's 35-by-90-foot pool is fed by the natural hot springs, and it is one of the largest private pools in Colorado. You can visit Waunita Hot Springs Ranch and enjoy it much more than Dr. Davis's patients ever did.

Waunita Hot Springs Ranch
8007 County Road 887
Gunnison, Colorado 81230
(970) 641-1266

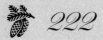

42 large, fresh mushrooms

1 pound Italian sausage

8 ounces cream cheese, softened

1 teaspoon dried red pepper, crushed

4½ cups flour

3 teaspoons baking powder

1½ teaspoons salt

1 teaspoon baking soda

¼ cup sugar

1 package dry yeast

¼ cup warm water

½ cup oil

2 cups lukewarm buttermilk

Sausage-Stuffed Mushrooms

Clean mushrooms and remove stems. Arrange in large baking dish. Cook sausage, stirring until done and crumbly. Drain. In a bowl, mix together sausage, cream cheese, and red pepper with electric mixer. Spoon mixture into mushroom caps. Bake at 350 degrees for 15 minutes. Serve immediately.

YIELD
Makes 3½ dozen

Angel Biscuits

Sift together flour, baking powder, salt, soda, and sugar. Set aside. Dissolve yeast in warm water. Add oil and buttermilk. Add dry ingredients to liquid and well. Knead lightly and place in greased bowl. Let rise about 30 minutes. Bake at 450 degrees about 15 minutes or until light brown.

YIELD
Makes 35 biscuits

Shrimp Scampi

Melt butter in saucepan. Add oil, garlic, parsley, lemon juice, mustard, and pepper. Mix well and simmer over low heat until garlic is soft. Add shrimp a few at a time and sauté over medium heat briefly until pink, tossing as they cook. Serve immediately.

YIELD

Serves 6

"Dinner, a time when . . . one should eat wisely but not too well, and talk well but not too wisely."

—W. Somerset Maugham

½ cup butter

¼ cup oil

4–6 cloves garlic, minced

¼ cup fresh parsley, minced

2 tablespoons lemon juice

½ teaspoon dry mustard

½ teaspoon black pepper

36 jumbo shrimp, cleaned

THE WYMAN HOTEL & INN

The Wyman Building

By Louis Wyman Jr.

Some buildings seem to reflect the personality of the men who built them. They endure the passing years with little change, honoring their builder's vision and strength. The Wyman building at Silverton, Colorado is just such an edifice. It pleases me, along with my older sister and younger brother—as it would have pleased my father—that his building, now well past the 75-year mark, will continue to be useful, with a hotel for tourists on the top floor.

My father, an emigrant from Germany, first came to Silverton about 1875. He was just a lad in his late teens. The only thing he owned at that time was the horse he rode. He had spent the previous winter in New Mexico, on Raton Pass, helping "Uncle Dick Wooten" with the winter traffic on his toll road. Wooten, no relation to my father, was a scout, trader, trapper and road builder. He was known as Uncle Dick throughout the Southwest.

In the spring of 1876 Louis Wyman Sr. headed for Silverton, Colorado—where, so he heard, you could shovel silver up off the streets. He found it wasn't quite that simple. During the ensuing years he went broke several times, trying to get a business started. But by 1887 he had together a fairly large freighting outfit and was handling all the supplies for the Silver Lake Mine.

By 1900 the aerial trams had been built. Pack mule teams and ore wagons were destined to fade from the scene. In a very short time this colorful period of the West's development slipped away into the pages and pictures of our history books. My father sold his entire freighting outfit to the British Government. Mules and pack saddles, six-horse teams, and wagons. Everything down to the manure forks and horseshoes. He trailed the outfit east to St. Louis, where everything was loaded onto river barges which made their way to New Orleans. From there, my father's freighting outfit went by ocean freighter to South Africa, where it was used to transport supplies for the British Army during the Boer War.

Once out of the freighting business, the senior Wyman turned his attention to real estate. In 1902 he built the Wyman Building on the same site where his old freighting office had been. The red sandstone for the masonry came from a quarry up South Mineral Creek. While the stonemasons were laying up the walls, he was cutting into two fine slabs of stone the image of his beloved pack mules. The finished pieces were set high on the facade of the building, where they remain to this day.

He planned his building to meet the needs of early-day Silverton. The old-timers had laid out the town with streets running north and south, east and west, true to the compass. Main Street running north and south seemed to divide the town in half. Both sides of Main Street were given over to the business district, and as many of Silverton's thirty-two saloons as there was room for. The east side of the town was the scene of a roaring nightlife common to every wide-open mining town. It was well equipped with dance halls and houses of pleasure, such as the Diamond Bell, The Bon Ton, The Laundry, The Tremont, The Ethiopian Temple of Pleasure and numerous others, where a gentleman out on a spree could find plenty of entertainment.

The west side was host to schools, churches and family homes. Whether this arrangement was planned or not, I don't know, but it worked out well. The main problem was that on the west side of town there were no buildings or halls where people could meet for parties or dances. So my father planned his building to take care of that need. At that time Silverton was an isolated mining town and its social life was centered around lodges and clubs. The Odd Fellows, The Moose, The Machabees, and The Woodsmen of the World. All of them were holding meetings wherever they could. And of course they couldn't dance in the churches. Most of the lodges had a chapter for their ladies, who also had their sewing circles and church organizations.

So my father designed the top floor of his building to take care of Silverton's social needs. A large part of the space was given over to a ballroom and lodge hall, with an adjoining banquet room. Both halls were well furnished and equipped with anterooms as well as a lounge for the ladies. For many years the top floor was busy with some activity almost every night.

Also upstairs were two three-room office suites that faced Main Street. These were usually occupied by dentists and mining companies. Dr. Baily, a dentist, had his office in the north suite for many years. He straightened my front teeth in that upstairs corner room. He was followed by doctors Morris, Finsilver, and Grouel. The south suite usually had one mining company or another as a tenant. They seemed to come and go every month or so. I got to know the tenants during my high school years when I helped out as a janitor, keeping the old steam boiler fired up to heat the place through the long winter months.

Finding tenants for the two large, street-level storerooms seemed a problem. McCrimmon Dry Goods and Ladies Wear occupied the south side for a number of years. The Silverton Electric Light Company moved in briefly, and some small businesses came and went, sometimes without paying their rent. The Silverton Commercial Club used the north side as a clubroom for a short time. But the storerooms never seemed to have an appeal as a business location.

With the demonetization of silver, the old mining town of Silverton was knocked to its knees. Many buildings on both sides of town stood empty and cold. As WWI wound down, base metals held the spotlight again and Silverton was able to hang on. The senior Wyman made one last effort to save his building by making a deal with the Graden Mercantile Company of Durango, Colorado. They were to bring a department store to Silverton—the town's first—occupying the entire upstairs floor.

When the remodeling was finished, the south room held a ladies furnishings and dry goods department. The archway between the two rooms was opened, and a grocery, meat market and bakery filled the north side. If Graden had stocked the store with new merchandise, he might have made it. But the people of Silverton weren't about to buy the bargain-basement and out-of-style goods the store offered. However, the grocery, meat market and bakery did a fair business. After a year or so, the department store folded and went back to Durango.

For many years after that, the building stood idle. The automobile and roads had come to the San Juans and Silverton was no longer an isolated mining camp. The town simply dropped its social life for the family car. But my father never stopped trying. It wasn't his nature to give up. But then a leg injury turned cancerous. On a black December day in 1924, we placed his coffin on a sled, drawn by a team of mules. A fitting cortege for his last trip.

After the senior Wyman's passing, D. M. Wyman, my younger brother, took up the battle to save the building, even mortgaging his home to pay the property tax and defeat a tax-title vulture trying to acquire the old edifice. I have always been grateful to Dave for making that effort. After settling the tax lien, he sold the building to Mr. Grant Gifford at a give-away price. It was the best deal he could hope for. Mr. Gifford used the downstairs rooms as a warm winter garage and storage for the crew that drove back and forth to the Mayflower Mine and Mill each day. The upstairs he converted into apartments. This arrangement lasted until the Mayflower Mine closed down.

The Wyman building then passed to several more owners in succession, each different and taking a toll from the sturdy old structure. The outlook at that time for the town was bleak. But then tourists discovered the San Juan country, and railroad buffs found the narrow gauge from Durango to Silverton. So Silverton and the Wyman Building have survived.

Mr. Don Stott acquired title to the old building and brought it back to something like its original condition, again accommodating public demand. The Wyman building became a Hotel, catering to the seasonal tourist trade. Today The Wyman Hotel & Inn is owned and operated by Rodger and Tana Wrublik in the spirit of the Old West. Its furnishings are indicative of the late 1800s and early 1900s. Louis Wyman Sr. would be proud that his building, despite the hard times it has survived, is still structurally sound. Like the town in which it has stood for more than three-quarters of a century, the building has a bright future. My father built well.

The Wyman Hotel & Inn
1371 Greene Street
PO Box 780
Silverton, Colorado 81433
(970) 387-5372

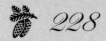

2 cups all-purpose flour

2 cups bread flour

4 tablespoons sugar

5 teaspoons baking powder

1 tablespoon baking soda

1 teaspoon sea salt

4 tablespoons cinnamon

4 large eggs, beaten

4 tablespoons butter, melted

4 cups buttermilk

2 Granny Smith apples, chopped fine

Granny Smith Apple Pancakes

Preheat griddle to about 375 degrees. Sift together all dry ingredients. Add eggs, butter, and milk and stir. Fold in chopped apples. Let mixture stand for 5 minutes.

Lightly butter a griddle and use about ⅓ cup batter per pancake. Bake for about 3 minutes or until top is bubbly. Turn over and bake for about the same amount of time.

 YIELD

Serves 6–8

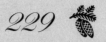

Pork Tenderloin
with Caramelized Balsamic Bermuda Onions

Wash tenderloins, dry with a paper towel, and set out at room temperature for about an hour to dry.

In a heavy skillet or wok, on medium-high heat, caramelize the onions in the butter and olive oil until light brown. Add balsamic vinegar and brown sugar, increase heat to high, and stir for 2 minutes. Remove from heat and add salt and pepper.

Rub tenderloins with olive oil and let sit for 10 minutes.

Preheat oven to 375 degrees. In a heavy skillet (we use a wok) on high heat, lightly sear the tenderloins on all sides. Place tenderloins in an oiled and covered roasting pan, arrange onion mixture over tenderloins, and roast until internal temperature is 150 degrees. Remove from oven and keep covered for at least 5 minutes. Carve slices across the grain about ¾ inch thick and drizzle onion and juices over tenderloin slices.

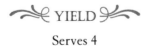
YIELD

Serves 4

two 1- to 1½-pound pork
    tenderloins

3 large Bermuda onions,
    halved and sliced very thin

2 tablespoons butter

2 tablespoons olive oil

⅓ cup balsamic vinegar

3 tablespoons dark brown sugar

¼ teaspoon sea salt

¼ teaspoon freshly ground
    black pepper

1 tablespoon extra virgin olive oil

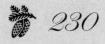

4 cups chicken stock

1 tablespoon olive oil

1 tablespoon unsalted butter

1 large red onion, thin sliced

5 cloves garlic, fine chopped

1½ pounds zucchini, coarsely chopped

14 ounces coconut milk

1 cup heavy cream

2 tablespoons curry powder

1 teaspoon ground cumin seed

salt and pepper to taste

chili sauce

Zucchini Curry Soup

In a heavy 4-quart saucepan over high heat, reduce stock to about 3 cups. In a heavy 6- or 8-quart stockpot, heat olive oil and butter over medium-high heat. Add onions and garlic; stir and sauté until transparent. Add zucchini; stir and cook covered for 2 minutes.

Add 1 cup of the reduced stock and simmer until zucchini is soft. Place zucchini in a food processor or blender and process until smooth. Place zucchini back into stockpot and heat over medium heat for 2 minutes. Add remainder of reduced stock and coconut milk and heavy cream. Continue to heat, not to boiling, and add curry powder and ground cumin seed. Stir and heat on low for 15–20 minutes, stirring every 5 minutes. Add salt and pepper to taste.

Serve in large bowls with a few dots of chili sauce on top.

Note: For an interesting change of flavor, eliminate the curry powder and ground cumin seed and substitute 1 teaspoon Thai red curry paste and 1 teaspoon Thai red chili paste. Dissolve the two pastes in about 1 cup of the hot stock and stir. Add slowly to soup while briskly stirring.

Bedouin Lamb

In a large stainless steel bowl, combine everything but the lamb. Blend well and add the lamb, stirring to coat evenly. Refrigerate for at least 6–8 hours, stirring occasionally to keep the lamb coated.

Remove the lamb from the marinade and pat dry with paper towels. Reserve the marinade. Thread the lamb cubes on long metal skewers and cook on a preheated, well-oiled grill for about 15 minutes. Turn lamb frequently, and brush with the reserved marinade.

Serve on a bed of rice with slivered almonds and walnuts.

Note: If you can get long-stemmed rosemary, use this in place of the metal skewers and reduce the rosemary in the marinade by 2 tablespoons.

¼ cup soy sauce

¼ cup extra virgin olive oil

¼ cup dry red wine

2 tablespoons lime juice

3 tablespoons fresh rosemary

1 teaspoon dark brown sugar

1½ pounds lean, boneless lamb, cut into 1-inch cubes

YIELD
Serves 4

"Wine brings to light the hidden secrets of the soul."

—Horace

South
Central

ANTLERS HILTON

Colorado Springs was an outgrowth of the Wild West atmosphere of Old Colorado City. When the Fifty-Niners descended on Colorado in 1859, seeking the fortunes in gold that were there to be found, several men established a typical mining town at the base of Pikes Peak. They incorporated themselves as the Colorado City Town Company on August 11, 1859.

Because the nearby Ute Pass was the quickest and best route to the South Park gold fields, the company located Colorado City on Fountain Creek, hoping to become the major mining supply town. Their foresight was rewarded. The new town prospered and was quickly filled with homes, boarding houses, supply stores, saloons, and houses of prostitution.

Almost as quickly, their fortunes and the prosperity of Colorado City began to decline. Competing routes to the gold fields diverted a lot of the traffic and business away from the area. But a good saloon in the Old West is a hard thing to kill, and the town hung on, attracting occasional visitors prospecting the area and serving residents who had given up on finding their fortunes in the mountains.

When General William Jackson Palmer arrived in Colorado in 1867, he was busy building railroads. He was already a railroad man before the Civil War started. Having studied railroad engineering and mining in Europe, he had seen in England how they burned coal instead of wood in their locomotives. Palmer is credited with bringing the practice to America.

Born in a Quaker family, Palmer was opposed to war. But he took a commission as a colonel in the Union Army when the Civil War broke out. Palmer was instrumental in forming the 15th Pennsylvania Volunteer Cavalry. In 1862, while scouting behind enemy lines prior to the Battle of Antietam, he was captured by the Confederates. Dressed in civilian clothes while gathering information for General George McClellan, Palmer could have been shot as a spy. Relying on his mining experience in Europe, he passed himself off as a mine owner, but the Confederates detained him anyway, incarcerating him at the Castle Thunder prison on Tobacco Row in Richmond, Virginia. After being released in a prisoner exchange, he rejoined his regiment in early 1863. When the war ended, he received the Medal of Honor and retired as a brigadier general.

Heading west with the railroads, Palmer became founder and president of the Denver and Rio Grande Railroad. When he first visited the region, he was very displeased with the drinking and debauchery that were part of everyday life in the mining town of Colorado City, although he was very impressed with the beauty of the surrounding area. He decided to establish an alcohol-free town near what is now called Old Colorado City.

General Palmer bought several hundred acres of land and incorporated it as Colorado Springs. He wanted to create a resort community featuring a luxury hotel and tree-lined boulevards. Thus, the first Antlers Hotel began welcoming guests in 1883. The Antlers soon became the center of the community, and development of the area followed. Under the direction of General Palmer, Colorado Springs remained "dry" until prohibition ended in 1929.

WWII saw the creation of Fort Carson as a training base. In 1954, President Eisenhower selected Colorado Springs as the site for the new Air Force Academy. Ironically, as the city grew, it incorporated Old Colorado City. Colorado Springs is now the second largest city in the state, and within its boundary lies the Garden of the Gods.

In an odd way, the naming of the garden reflects the atmosphere of both towns. When the Old Colorado City was first staked out in 1859, two men were exploring the area. While wandering through the astonishing rock formations, one commented that the spot "would be a capital place for a beer garden, when the country grew up." But the other protested and said, "Beer Garden! Why, it is a fit place for the Gods to assemble, and we will call it 'The Garden of the Gods.'"

Antlers Hilton
4 South Cascade Avenue
Colorado Springs, Colorado 80903
(719) 955-5600

2 tablespoons vegetable oil

6 pounds short ribs

1 onion

1 stalk celery

1 carrot

3 cloves garlic

1 tablespoon tomato paste

1 bottle Barolo wine

4 cups beef stock

2 sprigs thyme

2 sprigs rosemary

1 bay leaf

FOIE GRAS

½ pound foie gras

Barolo Braised Short Ribs
with Foie Gras

Pan-sear the short ribs until nicely caramelized. Add roughly cut vegetables and garlic to pan. Add tomato paste. Place all in oven for a half hour at 350 degrees.

Add wine, beef stock, and herbs and braise slowly for 3 hours.

Take the short ribs off the bone and present on farro (a high-protein wheat), or rice, or risotto.

FOIE GRAS

Slice foie gras in quarter-inch slices. Dust lightly in flour and sauté quickly in hot pan. Place on top of short ribs and serve.

"Tomatoes and oregano make it Italian; wine and tarragon make it French. Sour cream makes it Russian; lemon and cinnamon make it Greek. Soy sauce makes it Chinse; garlic makes it good."

—Alice May Brock

Onions Agrodolce

Peel onions. Place sugar, vinegar, and thyme in pan and cook until onions are caramelized and tender and liquid has evaporated.

1 pound pearl onions

1 cup sugar

1 cup cider vinegar

1 sprig thyme

Green Chili

Sauté pork with peppers and serrano chilies. Add chopped garlic and cover with flour. Cook mixture slowly for 10 minutes.

Add green chilies, chopped tomatoes, and chopped tomatillos. Add 1 gallon of water and cook slowly for 45 minutes.

Add cilantro and season with salt and pepper.

5 pounds pork loin, diced

2 cups chopped serrano chilies

2 cups diced peppers

1 cup chopped garlic

¼ cup flour

1 small can diced tomatoes

1 pound green chilies

12 fresh tomatillos

1 bunch cilantro, chopped

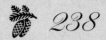 *238*

6 ounces beef fillet, totally
    cleaned

1 ounce blue cheese

1 ounce prosciutto, sliced
    very fine

1 tablespoon blackberries

2 tablespoons port wine

1 sprig rosemary

2 tablespoons basic brown sauce

Fillet of Beef Filled with Blue Cheese and Wrapped in Prosciutto

Make pocket in tenderloin and fill with blue cheese. Wrap in prosciutto and secure with a toothpick. Pan-sear tenderloin and place in moderate oven until desired doneness.

Deglaze with port wine, rosemary, and blackberries. Add brown sauce and serve.

B & E FILLING STATION

The first inhabitants in this area were the Mountain Ute, Arapaho, Kiowa, and Cheyenne Indian tribes. Their attraction to the area was partly responsible for the white man's coming. It was apparent that abundant fish and game were available, and the fact that Native Americans enjoyed living in the area was inducement enough to encourage white settlers.

In 1820, U.S. Army Major Stephen Long led an expedition through here. When traveling between Palmer Lake and Monument, his group was the first to identify and record the columbine, which has since become the state flower of Colorado.

As trappers, fur traders, and prospectors opened the area to development, homesteaders and ranchers began to settle the land. David McShane and Henry Limbach brought their families and helped create Monument, which served as a commercial center for the area. Several gold mines were dug, but no very large deposits were found.

Following the Civil War, General William Jackson Palmer was given the job of building the Kansas Pacific Railroad from St. Louis to Denver. In the process, he saw a beautiful spot that he eventually helped incorporate as Colorado Springs. The Kansas Pacific Railroad was only funded to reach Denver, so General Palmer found financing and built his own 3-foot, narrow-gauge railroad to continue down the front range of the mountains. When Colorado Springs welcomed the Denver and Rio Grande Railroad in 1871, it set off rapid development of the area. Palmer Lake was critical to the railroad because the steam trains labored hard to reach the summit and needed to take on water. The lake was the only natural water supply available.

Dr. William Finley Thompson, a dentist from Baltimore, was practicing in Denver. After seeing Palmer Lake, he purchased land and laid out the new town in 1882, planning to develop it as a health resort and vacation community. Thompson built the Victorian mansion, Estemere, in 1887 for his family. Palmer Lake became a destination for Denver residents anxious to escape the city. The Rocky Mountain Chautauqua was active in the area from 1887 to 1910, hosting programs in music, art, drama, religion, and nature.

Winter offered plenty of cold weather, and ice harvesting became an ongoing business for a time. Fox farms, sawmills, Angora rabbit raising, and farming rounded out the commercial aspects of Palmer Lake. More recently, the Air Force Academy, opened in 1958, has given the town a real economic boost.

The B & E Filling Station has been a local eating favorite for many years. (The *B* is for Bohler, and the *E* is for Elliott.) The Bohlers and Elliots were the original partners, but Mike and Ingrid Elliott left in 2000. The name was retained, and Chris and Kerri Bohler still own and manage the facility. Chris is the chef, and Kerri oversees the dining room. They have both been in the restaurant business for over 25 years. Their stated goal is to provide customers with the best value possible.

Chris's philosophy of food is to use the best ingredients available with unique flavor combinations and presentations to create incredible dishes. Kerri's philosophy about attention to detail is to always give great service unobtrusively while making customers feel comfortable.

B & E Filling Station
25 South Highway 105
Palmer Lake, Colorado 80133
(719) 481-4780

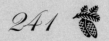

Green Eggs and Ham

Place all ingredients in a nonstick skillet. Over medium heat, stir constantly with a rubber spatula until eggs are cooked, spinach is wilted, and cheese is melted. Cooking time is about 3 to 4 minutes. Serve with your favorite potatoes.

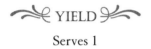 YIELD

Serves 1

1 ounce clarified butter

2 beaten eggs, scrambled

1 large avocado, diced

¾ cup fresh baby spinach

2 ounces ham, diced

¼ cup shredded smoked Gouda

3–5 precooked pancakes using
your favorite recipe, but let
pancakes cool

2 eggs

1 cup half-and-half

½ teaspoon vanilla extract

ORANGE MAPLE SYRUP

¼ cup orange juice, freshly
squeezed

½ cup pure maple syrup

Autumn Cakes

*These wonderful pancakes are named after a great em-
ployee who suggested them. We serve either 3 or 5 cakes per
person.*

In a bowl, combine eggs, half-and-half, and vanilla extract. Dip pancakes in egg and cream mixture and
place on hot griddle with melted butter. Cook 1 to 2
minutes on each side. Serve topped with orange maple
syrup.

ORANGE MAPLE SYRUP

Heat orange juice and syrup together in a sauce pan.
Serve over pancakes and sprinkle with powdered
sugar. Serve with butter.

YIELD
Serves 1

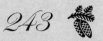

Grilled Portobello Focaccia

Place all ingredients on top of one another, starting with mushrooms. Cover with a lid and grill for about 2 to 3 minutes. Place ingredients on focaccia bread and slice.

 YIELD

Serves 1

1 piece focaccia bread, cut in half and lightly grilled

3 ounces portobello mushrooms, sliced and grilled

2 tablespoons roasted red bell pepper, diced

½ cup fresh baby spinach

¼ cup smoked Gouda cheese, shredded

THE BRO^ADMOOR

The BRO^ADMOOR had its beginning in 1880, when Willie Wilcox, who came to the area seeking his fortune and hoping to find a cure for his tuberculosis, bought the land. Willie established a small dairy, but unfortunately his inexperience with animals soon became evident. He realized that without significant investments the project would not be a success, so he began negotiations to sell the land.

A Prussian Count, James Pourtales, had also come to Colorado seeking romance and fortune. In 1885 he brought his knowledge of German scientific farming to Colorado Springs and entered into a partnership with Wilcox to bring the Broadmoor Dairy Farm back to life. Although the dairy was still doing well by 1888, Pourtales decided it would not return enough profit to be of aid to his estates in Prussia. He revamped his business plans and decided to create an upper-class suburb of Colorado Springs with numerous amenities to increase the value of the home sites.

In 1890, the count formed the Broadmoor Land and Investment Company and purchased the original 2,400-acre tract. To entice buyers, Pourtales erected The Broadmoor Casino, which opened July 1, 1891. A small hotel was also constructed a few years later. Continually beset by financial difficulties, Pourtales was unsuccessful in developing the site, and the property was forced into receivership. The casino and the small neighboring hotel were used for many local events, but they were eventually converted into a boarding house and day school for girls.

In 1916, Spencer Penrose, a Philadelphia capitalist who had made a fortune in gold and copper mining, acquired The Broadmoor Casino and Hotel 40-acre site, and an adjoining 400 acres. Penrose intended to turn the Pikes Peak region into the most interesting, multifaceted resort area that could be imagined, and he had the money to make it happen.

Using New York architects, Penrose began construction of the main complex on May 20, 1917. With the objective of creating the most beautiful resort in the world, Spencer Penrose imported artisans from Italy and other European countries to create the ornate moldings and paintings that adorn the interior of The BRO^ADMOOR as well as the elaborate exterior detailing. Italian Renaissance in style, the original BRO^ADMOOR resort was designed with four wings, which were completed in June 1918. An 18-hole golf course was designed by Donald Ross, a master golf-course architect of the era.

Officially opened on June 29, 1918, the resort was christened The BRO^ADMOOR. Architectural and design features included a spectacular curved marble staircase, dramatic chandeliers, Della

Robbia–style tile, hand-painted beams and ceilings, a carved marble fountain, and a striking pink stucco façade.

Spencer Penrose was equally brilliant in promoting and marketing not only the resort, but the surrounding areas. He correctly assessed the tourist value of Pikes Peak for the growth of The BRO^ADMOOR, and he built the Pikes Peak Road leading to the summit as an alternative to the cog railway. He also established the Cheyenne Mountain Zoo, still considered one of the finest privately owned zoos in the United States. In 1925, Penrose purchased and modernized the Pikes Peak Cog Railway, which became one of his most enduring legacies.

The BRO^ADMOOR quickly became one of the finest resorts of its time, attracting "captains of industry" and dignitaries from around the world. It was considered the "European alternative," and many visitors, following the same attraction that brought early settlers, came for the clean mountain air that was said to relieve symptoms of tuberculosis and other bronchial maladies.

When The BRO^ADMOOR first opened under Penrose in 1918, he charged every employee with providing a level of service and overall experience as yet unavailable in the United States, but expected throughout Europe. He brought in Italian Executive Chef Louis Stratta and charged him with bringing his inventive and international ideas to America's West.

The BRO^ADMOOR's surge in fame led to an expansion of the resort's facilities. Addressing the popularity of golf, famed golf course architect Robert Trent Jones was enlisted to design a second golf course, which was expanded to 18 holes in 1965. A third course, designed by Ed Seay and Arnold Palmer, was added in 1976.

Over the years, additional facilities were added, including more than 300 new guest rooms, the Penrose Room, a fine dining restaurant, and The BRO^ADMOOR Spa, Golf and Tennis Club. Extensive renovations have brought even the oldest portion of the property up to date with modern plumbing and high-tech safety features.

This grand resort has been the destination of presidents, statesmen, foreign dignitaries, and celebrities. Presidents Hoover, Franklin Roosevelt, Eisenhower, Kennedy, Nixon, Ford, Reagan, George H.W. Bush, and George W. Bush have all stayed at The BRO^ADMOOR. Foreign dignitaries have included King Hussein of Jordan, Princess Anne, Prime Minister Toshiki Kaifu of

Japan, the King of Siam, and Margaret Thatcher. Other notable guests have been John Wayne, Maurice Chevalier, Bing Crosby, Walt Disney, Charles Lindbergh, Clark Gable, Bob Hope, Jimmy Stewart, Jack Benny, Jackie Gleason, Sir Elton John, Peggy Fleming, Joe DiMaggio, Stan Musial, Stephen Tyler and Aerosmith, and Michael Douglas.

The BRO^ADMOOR
1 Lake Avenue
Colorado Springs, Colorado 80906
(719) 577-5775
(866) 837-9520

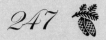

BROADMOOR
Bread Pudding
with Vanilla Sauce

Preheat oven to 325 degrees. Butter one 12-by-18-by-2½-inch glass pan; set aside.

Place milk, eggs, and sugar in mixing bowl. Mix on low speed until smooth. Add spices, salt, and vanilla to mix.

Layer prepared pan with French bread sliced to ¼ inch thick. Sprinkle raisins over the bread. Pour milk mixture over evenly. Bake in a water bath for 40 to 45 minutes. Custard should be set.

VANILLA SAUCE

Combine the egg yolks and sugar in a mixing bowl. Whip until light and fluffy. In saucepot, bring half-and-half to the scalding point with the vanilla bean. Remove the bean, cut in half, and scrape out vanilla puree. Place puree in saucepot with hot cream and mix well.

Add ¼ cup of hot cream to the yolk mixture, stirring quickly to temper. Gradually add the remaining cream while stirring rapidly. Place the mixture over simmering

1 quart whole milk

6 eggs, beaten

3 egg yolks, beaten

¾ cup granulated sugar

1 teaspoon cinnamon

¾ teaspoon nutmeg, freshly grated

¼ teaspoon allspice

½ teaspoon salt

1 teaspoon vanilla extract

1½ pounds French bread, ¼-inch slices with crust left on

1½ cups raisins

VANILLA SAUCE

12 egg yolks

1¼ cups granulated sugar

1 quart half-and-half

1 vanilla bean

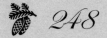

water and heat slowly. Stir constantly until it is thick enough to coat the back of a spoon. Be very careful not to heat over 190 degrees, as it will curdle. Chill.

TO SERVE

Serve bread pudding warm with vanilla sauce poured over or on the side. Add fresh berries and whipped cream for garnish.

YIELD

Serves 15

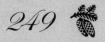

BROADMOOR
Charles Court Pepper Steak

Sauté filet until it reaches desired doneness, and set aside.

To the hot sauté pan with a fond (browned and caramelized bits of meat from cooking), add the shallots, mustard, peppercorns, and chutney. Stir briskly and bring to a boil. Remove from heat and add brandy. Ignite and burn off. When the flame has died down, add the demi-glace and bring to a boil. Add the cream and adjust the seasoning with salt and a few drops of lemon.

YIELD
Serves 1

6 ounces center-cut filet mignon

SAUCE

2 shallots, diced

3 teaspoons Dijon mustard

1 pinch cracked green
      peppercorns

1 pinch cracked black
      peppercorns

½ cup chutney

2 ounces brandy

3 cups demi-glace

¼ cup heavy cream

salt to taste

½ fresh lemon

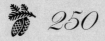

1½ pounds American cheese

6 tablespoons butter

⅓ cup mayonnaise

1½ teaspoons Worcestershire

¼ teaspoon Tabasco

1⅓ teaspoons sherry

2 teaspoons dry mustard

1⅓ tablespoons lemon juice

Golden Bee Cheese Dip

Put butter and half of the cheese in food processor. Pulse for about 5 minutes. Add remaining cheese, plus other ingredients and mix until smooth. *Do not over-mix*, or the cheese will break down.

⊱ YIELD ⊰
Serves 8

THE CLIFF HOUSE

The gold mines in the Pikes Peak area spawned the town of Manitou Springs in the late 1850s. What began as a stagecoach stop on the route from Colorado Springs to Leadville turned into a 20-room boarding house known as "The Inn." It was one of the most popular stagecoach runs of the American West. Many trappers and hunters on their way to or from Colorado Springs were drawn to the inviting parlors and rambling porches of the inn. When the mines in Leadville proved profitable, many capitalists made their way through Manitou Springs, bringing more business to the small inn. At times tents had to be pitched outside to accommodate the overflow of guests.

As the gold in the Pikes Peak region began to play out, travel through the area dwindled, and by 1876 The Inn was struggling to find guests. Luckily, over the next half-dozen years, interest in the town's ancient mineral springs was beginning to increase. The springs bubbled up from underground limestone aquifers that carbonated the water and infused it with minerals. The water was cool, good-tasting, and had a high concentration of minerals that many believed benefited the body. American Indians had been drinking it straight from the springs for hundreds of years, believing that it offered healing powers.

In the 1870s, Edward E. Nichols came west to fight a battle with tuberculosis. Having beaten the illness, Nichols settled permanently in Manitou Springs, a town where he served as mayor for eight terms. He bought The Inn in 1886, renaming it The Cliff House and turning it into a refined resort hotel that capitalized on the sparkling waters and mineral springs in the region.

In 1914, Nichols teamed up with Colorado Governor Shoup to found the Manitou Bath House Company. They turned the struggling community into an entire resort specializing in water therapies. The Cliff House at Pikes Peak generated a sudden influx of wealthy clients eager to take advantage of the healing powers of the springs. The hotel became a popular resort for the wealthy and remained in style well into the 20th century. Over the 30 years following the founding of the Manitou Bath House Company, Nichols expanded the property from 20 to 56 rooms, and eventually to 200. The end result was the beautiful, four-and-a-half-story building that stands today.

The Cliff House at Pikes Peak was a popular destination for the wealthy and influential. Guests included Teddy Roosevelt; Ferdinand, Crown Prince of Austria; Charles Dickens Jr.; P. T. Barnum; Thomas Edison; Clark Gable; F. W. Woolworth; and J. Paul Getty. Every guest of The Cliff House received the personalized attention expected at a premier resort hotel. Each evening, guests could enjoy formal dinners and then retire to concerts on the grounds. After enjoying the entertainment, guests were encouraged to cross the street to the Soda Springs spa for a glass of fresh spring water

before retiring. The Cliff House at Pikes Peak even created underground tunnels from the hotel to the spa.

Eventually, a bathhouse was built at the spa, and bellboys from the hotel would cross to the spring to fill bottles and glasses with the sparkling water for the guests. The Cliff House soon became the most popular destination in the Colorado Springs region. But even after all its successes, The Cliff House at Pikes Peak occasionally suffered some hard times. A flash flood roared down Williams Canyon in 1921 and washed through the hotel's Grill Room.

California real estate developer James S. Morley purchased The Cliff House at Pikes Peak in 1981, and he quickly turned the historic building into a 42-unit apartment building. But in March 1982, the building caught fire, and the roof sustained so much damage it had to be replaced. Also, the interior was stripped of all plumbing, plaster, and floor coverings. Water damage was so extensive, the very survival of the building was threatened. Action was taken to preserve what remained; but when the economy declined, the building stood vacant for 16 years.

In 1997, Morley committed to the restoration of the old inn. He vowed to restore the hotel to its original distinction and fame, preserving the Rocky Mountain Victorian architecture of the 1800s but incorporating 21st-century state-of-the-art technology and amenities. Today's fabulous Cliff House at Pikes Peak is the result of his personal efforts and vision.

The Cliff House at Pikes Peak
306 Cañon Avenue
Manitou Springs, Colorado 80829
(888) 212-7000
(719) 685-3000

Sweet Corn Bisque

In a large soup pot on high heat, sauté leeks and onions until soft with just a little color. Add corn and continue to cook for about 10–15 minutes on medium heat. Next, add the flour to the leek, onion, and corn mixture. This is going to thicken the mixture almost to a paste. Continue to cook for about 5 minutes. Add chicken stock and bring to a boil, then lower the heat and simmer for 15–20 minutes. Using a hand blender, puree the soup until smooth. Continue blending; add cream gradually, almost like you are emulsifying the soup. Place back on the stove and bring it to a simmer. Run the soup through a fine mesh strainer. Season with salt and pepper. The garnish is really up to you; this soup goes great with lobster, smoked chicken, grilled squash, and any aromatic herbs.

½ pound butter

1 cup all-purpose flour

3 medium yellow onions, diced small

3 leeks, diced small

8 cups corn kernels

6 cups chicken stock

3 cups heavy cream

salt and pepper to taste

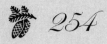

eight 5- to 6-ounce duck breasts

1 cup olive oil

1½ cups Grand Marnier

1 tablespoon sherry vinegar

1 tablespoon sugar

3 oranges, juiced

3 peeled oranges, in segments

salt and pepper

Orange Duck
(duck à l'orange)

In a large sauté pan on high heat, add the oil. Score the fat side of each duck breast with a chef's knife. Season the duck with salt and pepper and some sugar. As soon as the sauté pan is hot, add the duck breast fat side down, lower the heat to medium, and baste the duck with the oil and juices that are coming out for 8–10 minutes. Add 1½ cups Grand Marnier and set aside to let the duck rest for 5 minutes.

Remove the duck from the pan but keep it warm. To the pan, add 1 tablespoon sherry vinegar, 1 tablespoon sugar, and juice from 3 oranges. Place pan back on the stove and reduce these ingredients to make the sauce. Pour sauce through a fine strainer and place back on the stove. Add the orange segments to the sauce. Serve separately in a gravy boat.

Veal Napoleon

Peel the potatoes and discard the skins. Add potatoes to other ingredients, then put in mixer and knead with the dough hook until incorporated but not beyond. Remove dough from mixer and separate into four pieces. On a lightly floured surface, take each piece and roll into a long, thin tube about ½ inch in diameter. Once all the dough is rolled out, slice the dough every 1 inch, creating small cylinders. Boil the gnocchi in lightly salted rapidly boiling water for 4 minutes, or until they rise to the top of the water. Remove the gnocchi and place on towels to dry. Heat up a small sauté pan, add 2 tablespoons of butter, and sauté the gnocchi till golden brown. Remove from pan and set aside in a warm place.

Lightly salt and pepper the veal cutlets, then dredge in flour. Sauté in medium sauté pan with about a tablespoon of oil until lightly browned, about 1 minute per side. Set aside on towel to drain off fat.

Place uncooked lobster in the same pan and pour Madeira into pan to deglaze.

Add Madeira wine sauce, then place in oven for 4–5 minutes or until lobster is cooked.

2 tablespoons butter

two 3-ounce veal cutlets

½ cup flour

1 tablespoon oil

1½ ounces lobster meat

1 cup Madeira wine

two 2-ounce slices of Gruyère cheese (robust, aged Swiss cheese)

12 grilled asparagus tips

POTATO GNOCCHI

2 cups flour

1 egg

7 potatoes, baked for 1 hour at 350 degrees

salt and pepper to taste

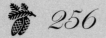

TO SERVE

Place 5–6 gnocchi around entire rim of plate, place 1 piece of veal in center of plate, put lobster with sauce directly on top of veal. Place one slice of Gruyère over lobster and repeat for the second plate. Garnish with asparagus tips.

YIELD

Serves 2

Chateaubriand Marinade

Mix together the orange juice, balsamic vinegar, sugar, and chili sauce. Use as a marinade for beef tenderloin (we use an 8-ounce portion of the thickest part of the tenderloin). Allow the meat to marinate overnight.

CHATEAU POTATOES

Boil potatoes and strain. Melt butter in cream and add to potatoes. Whip together with all ingredients.

SAUTÉED NEW POTATOES

Boil new potatoes until fork tender. Sauté in oil with bacon and shallots.

⚞ YIELD ⚟
Makes 1 quart

1 cup orange juice

1 cup balsamic vinegar

1 cup sugar

3 tablespoons sweet chili sauce (hot pepper sauce found at Asian markets)

CHATEAU POTATOES

5 pounds Yukon potatoes

½ pound butter

1 quart heavy cream

½ pound bacon

1 cup diced red and yellow peppers

½ cup chopped chives

½ cup chopped artichoke hearts

½ cup sour cream

salt, pepper, and garlic to taste

SAUTÉED NEW POTATOES

2 pounds new potatoes

4 strips bacon

3 tablespoons diced shallots

2 tablespoons olive oil

RAINBOW TROUT RANCH

One result of the mass migration of prospectors and miners to Colorado in the last half of the 19th century was the coming of the railroads. Antonito, named after the San Antonio River and mountains in the area, was the site of one of the train depots. The Denver and Rio Grande Railroad depot located in the heart of Antonito was built of hand-hewn lava rock in 1880.

After the D&RG was absorbed by the Union Pacific Railroad, it continued to operate from the depot for years. The depot was given back to the city recently and continues to function as a museum for the D&RG and as the depot for the Cumbres and Toltec Scenic Railroad that travels from Antonito to Chama, New Mexico. The nearby town of Conejos boasts the oldest church in Colorado, Our Lady of Guadelupe Church.

Sometime during the late 1880s, Tommy Johnson homesteaded on the Conejos River approximately 25 miles west of Antonito, Colorado. He and his family ran the spread as a cattle ranch. In the early 1920s, Dr. Taylor of New Orleans explored the South San Juan Mountains. Recognizing the beauty and loving the fishing available, he organized the Conejos Rainbow Trout Lodges Association. He sold ownership shares to investors, including the movie actor Douglas Fairbanks Sr.

The association expanded in 1921 by buying the Tommy Johnson property. By 1925 the project was not going well. Dr. Taylor went to Dallas to drum up business and met W. B. Hamilton, president of the Texhoma Oil Company of Wichita Falls, Texas. Hamilton put a group of buyers together and took control of the property just as fire destroyed the old dining hall.

Hamilton had seen a Bavarian hunting lodge in Europe and contracted with an architect to reproduce the structure on the site of the old dining hall. The new lodge included living quarters, a spacious kitchen and pantries, and more than 5,000 square feet of dining and sitting room area, separated by a double-faced stone fireplace. The ceiling rises to 40 feet, offering a dramatic eating environment in the Colorado wilderness.

The lodge is surrounded on three sides by a porch that has offered years of cool mountain breezes. Decorated with a number of feeders, the porch offers rocking chairs you can park yourself in and watch as dozens of hummingbirds all feed at the same time. When it was first built, the lodge was one of the largest log buildings of its kind in the West. Electricity was provided by a water-powered turbine generator located on La Manga Creek, across the valley from the ranch site. Tents were replaced by 19 log cabins, some offering two bedrooms and others with sitting rooms and fireplaces.

The ranch stayed in the Hamilton family for several decades. Bill Hamilton bought the property from his parents and operated it with his wife, Shirley, until it was sold in 1992 to Jim Gordon from Tumbling River Ranch and Doug and Linda Van Berkum. Together, they changed the name to Rainbow Trout Ranch and completely refurbished the place. Their combined experience in running guest ranches has produced an opportunity for families to really experience what it means to live in wilderness comfort.

The fishing is excellent, the horseback riding is breathtaking along the mountain trails, and the food is outstanding. Spectacular scenery abounds everywhere. Faith, Hope, and Charity, the rock formations that serve as the backdrop for the ranch, are enjoyed from the comfortable porch.

The Van Berkums still manage the ranch. In deference to the Hamilton family's vision, the Van Berkums wish to continue the tradition of offering guests a great ranch experience in the Conejos River Valley.

Rainbow Trout Ranch
1484 FDR 250
PO Box 458
Antonito, Colorado 81120
(800) 633-3397
(719) 376-5659

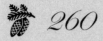
3 eggs

1½ cups milk

1 cup oil

2 cups sugar

3 cups flour

1½ teaspoons salt

1½ teaspoons baking powder

1½ tablespoons poppy seed

1½ teaspoons vanilla extract

1½ teaspoons almond extract

GLAZE

¼ cup orange juice

¼ cup sugar

½ teaspoon vanilla extract

½ teaspoon almond extract

Poppy-Seed Bread

In an electric mixer, blend the eggs, milk, oil, and sugar. Add flour, salt, and baking powder. Add poppy seeds and the vanilla and almond extracts. Mix for 1–2 minutes more.

Grease bread pans. Pour in bread batter. (To remove any air bubbles in the batter, drag a knife through each pan before baking, or tap the pans on a table.) Bake 1 hour at 350 degrees.

Optional: Drizzle loaves with glaze if desired (recipe follows).

GLAZE

Combine all ingredients and boil 1–2 minutes. Spread over warm loaves.

YIELD
Makes 2 loaves

Peach Cobbler

This is a high-altitude recipe to cook in a Dutch oven over a campfire.

Melt the butter in a Dutch oven. Then put in a thin layer of batter, topped with half of fruit. Repeat these layers, ending with batter.

Set the Dutch oven in hot coals, and pack them around the Dutch oven and on top of the lid. Cook until done (30–45 minutes, depending on the heat of the coals).

Serve with sugar and cream. (If using peaches above, add 1 cup of sugar to pour over fruit before cooking.)

 YIELD

Serves 6–8

1 cup butter

4 cups sliced peaches, drained, rinsed and quartered (or 4 cups apple pie filling)

BATTER

1 cup sugar

3 cups flour

4 teaspoons baking powder

1 teaspoon salt

1 cup milk

1 teaspoon almond extract (for peaches) or 1 teaspoon each of vanilla and cinnamon (for apples)

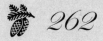

4 tomatoes, sliced or wedged

½ red onion, diced

3 zucchini, thinly sliced

DRESSING

1⅓ cups olive oil

½ cup red wine vinegar

¼ cup Parmesan cheese, grated

1 tablespoon sugar

2 teaspoons salt

1 teaspoon celery salt

½ teaspoon white pepper

½ teaspoon dry mustard

¼ teaspoon paprika

1 garlic clove, minced

Tomato-Zucchini-Onion Salad

Place vegetables together in large bowl. In a separate bowl, combine dressing ingredients and mix well. Chill.

Just before serving, mix dressing well and add to salad. You may not have to use all of the dressing; just use enough to coat the vegetables.

YIELD
Serves 8–12

"There is no such thing as a little garlic."

— Anonymous

ROYAL GORGE ROUTE RAILROAD

As with most sites in Colorado, the earliest recorded humans living in this area were Native Americans. The Ute often spent winters in the Cañon City area, eventually attracting the Sioux, Cheyenne, Kiowa, Blackfoot, and Comanche as they followed the buffalo herds into the mountain meadows. Spanish explorers recorded their visits to this region as early as 1642. As white men came to trap and trade furs in the 1700s, they encouraged more serious discovery.

Lt. Zebulon Pike stopped here and set up a camp from which his group could explore the nearby gorge in 1806. His expedition became so famous that Pikes Peak was named in his honor.

The Royal Gorge meant little to anyone until 1877, when silver was discovered upriver in the Arkansas valley. The resulting flood of prospectors and miners also brought the railroads. And competition between the railroads sparked a conflict known as the Royal Gorge War. The Rio Grande and the Santa Fe both wanted the rights to build a new freight line to carry ore down from the mountains.

Just west of Cañon City, the Arkansas River has cut through a high rock plateau forming a spectacular steep-walled gorge more than 1,000 feet deep. Its narrowest point is about 30 feet wide, and steep walls on both sides plunge into the river. This gorge was a tremendous barrier for the railroads. The valley could accommodate two railroads in most places, but in some sections only one set of tracks could be laid. Crews from the Santa Fe and the Denver and Rio Grande literally fought over the right to build.

The Santa Fe hired legendary gunfighter and U.S. Marshal Bat Masterson and his Kansas posse to help protect their crew and materials, while the Rio Grande employed a 200-man posse led by former Governor A. C. Hunt. An extended period of sabotage and murder culminated in a long court battle. The local battle ended in 1879, when the U.S. Supreme Court granted the D&RG primary rights to build through the gorge.

The war continued as the Santa Fe decided to compete with D&RG in other locations. Fearing financial ruin, the creditors for D&RG forced management to lease the rights to the Santa Fe, which completed the track through the gorge. Then the great financier, Jay Gould, entered the contest, pledging $400,000 to the D&RG to compete with the Santa Fe in other routes. More local fighting resulted in the "Treaty of Boston," which gave the route back to the D&RG. The line eventually reached the great silver mines of Leadville in 1880.

The Santa Fe Railroad is credited with building the famous hanging bridge. At a point where the gorge narrows to just 30 feet, the railroad was suspended over the river along the north side. Here sheer rock walls extend down into the river on both sides. C. Shallor Smith, a Kansas engineer, designed a 175-foot plate girder that is suspended on one side by steel "A" frame girders spanning the river and anchored to the rock walls. When built in 1879, the bridge cost $11,759, a huge sum back then. Although it had to be strengthened over the years, this unique structure has served on a main rail line for nearly 130 years.

Passenger service began in 1880. In 1882 the Royal Gorge route became a transcontinental rail link between Denver and Salt Lake. The Royal Gorge, where the canyon walls rise 2,600 feet above the tracks, became known as the Grand Canyon of the Arkansas River. Passenger trains have stopped at this point for decades to allow passengers to alight and marvel at the sights and sounds of nature and see how man had conquered one of nature's obstacles.

At one point, four transcontinental passenger trains a day passed through the Royal Gorge. Modern transportation eventually shut down this route, and it is now used for scenic tourist rides. You can access the Royal Gorge Route train in Cañon City at the Santa Fe Depot.

Cañon City is on Highway 50, along the Arkansas River at the mouth of the Royal Gorge. It was originally developed as a supply depot during the Pikes Peak gold rush in 1859. Alferd Packer, one of only three people convicted of murder and cannibalism in America, was imprisoned in Cañon City. Local tradition says that at Packer's first trial, the Democratic judge told him, "There were seven Democrats in Hinsdale County and you ate five of them."

Royal Gorge Route
Historic Santa Fe Depot
401 Water Street
Cañon City, Colorado 81212
(888) 724-5748
(303) 569-1000

Seafood Gumbo

Sauté garlic, onion, celery, and bell pepper with butter and olive oil in a large stockpot until ingredients start to caramelize and stick to bottom of pot. Add white wine to deglaze pan and simmer 1 minute.

Add tomatoes, okra, seasonings, chicken stock, and water and bring to a boil. Cover, reduce heat, and simmer 10 minutes.

Add lobster, crab, shrimp, and rice and simmer an additional 5 minutes. Salt to taste.

2 tablespoons butter

4 tablespoons olive oil

2 cloves garlic, minced

2 large sweet yellow onions, chopped

4 stalks celery, diced

¼ cup finely minced red and/or yellow bell pepper

1 cup dry white wine

6 medium fresh tomatoes, chopped

10 ounces frozen okra

¼ teaspoon white pepper

¼ teaspoon crushed red pepper

2 teaspoons black pepper

1 tablespoon thyme

1 tablespoon Old Bay Seasoning

1 tablespoon dried cilantro

6 cups chicken broth

6 cups water

6 ounces lobster meat

6 ounces crabmeat

8 ounces small shrimp, shelled and deveined

2 cups cooked white rice

four 6- to 7-ounce duck breasts

4 ounces thinly sliced prosciutto

4 slices smoked Gouda cheese

3 cloves chopped garlic

one 6-ounce package frozen
    or fresh spinach

1 cup all-purpose flour

1 cup panko bread crumbs

1 egg

1 cup water

salt and pepper to taste

vegetable, canola, or corn oil

Duck Breast Pinwheels

Heat sauté pan with 2 tablespoons oil and add garlic. Cook about 2 minutes, then add spinach and cook until wilted. Remove from heat and allow to cool. Put spinach in a colander and press out excess liquid with your hand. Set aside.

Remove skin and trim duck breasts to remove tendons. Place breasts between two sheets of heavy-duty plastic wrap and pound with meat hammer to flatten into a squarish shape of consistent thickness, being careful not to create holes.

Lay breasts out flat, skin side down. Add thin, even layers of spinach, prosciutto, and Gouda cheese. Starting at the bottom edge, roll breasts into logs and secure with toothpicks. Beat together egg and water in a small bowl. Lightly flour duck rolls, dip in egg mixture, and roll in panko crumbs on a separate plate.

In a frying pan, pour oil about ½ inch deep. Heat to medium high and gently place duck rolls into oil. Turn over to evenly brown breadcrumb coating. Do not fully cook. Remove to drain on paper towels.

In a 350-degree preheated oven, bake duck rolls for 20 minutes in a shallow dish. Remove and allow to cool for 5 minutes. Cut rolls into 4 or 5 pinwheels each and serve as a main dish or for appetizers.

Elk Tenderloin Medallions au Poivre

Evenly season elk with half of the salt, marjoram, and thyme. Bring a large sauté pan to high heat with olive oil and butter. When the oil and butter mixture starts to smoke, add elk medallions and quickly sear each side; remove to a plate and set aside.

In the same pan, add shallots and garlic; sauté until they caramelize and begin sticking to the bottom. Add red wine and agitate pan; reduce the sauce to half. Add veal demi-glace, black pepper, and the remaining thyme and marjoram. Bring to a boil, then reduce heat and simmer uncovered for about 5 minutes. Add elk to reheat, about 2 minutes, and serve.

twelve 2-ounce pieces elk tenderloin, pounded flat

2 cups veal demi-glace or beef stock

2 medium shallots, minced

4 cloves garlic, minced

2 tablespoons crushed black pepper crushed

1 teaspoon salt

1 teaspoon dried marjoram

½ teaspoon dried thyme

1 cup full-bodied red wine (Cabernet Sauvignon)

2 tablespoons olive oil

4 tablespoons butter

LAMB CHOPS

four 5-ounce lamb chops

2 tablespoons dried marjoram

2 tablespoons dried thyme

2 tablespoons rosemary

2 tablespoons black pepper

salt to taste

3 tablespoons olive oil

2 tablespoons butter

WILD RICE PILAF

one 10-ounce bag frozen
    shelled edamame

one 16-ounce package
    wild rice blend

2 cups chopped parsnips

1 medium onion, chopped

2 stalks celery, chopped

1 teaspoon celery salt

1 tablespoon garlic powder

1 tablespoon onion powder

2 tablespoons chopped parsley

1 tablespoon dried thyme

1 tablespoon dried summer
    savory

salt and pepper to taste

chicken broth (about 2–3 cups)

Roasted Herbed Lamb Chops
with Parsnip and Edamame Wild Rice Pilaf

LAMB CHOPS

Season lamb chops with a mixture of marjoram, thyme, rosemary, salt, and pepper. In a hot pan, add olive oil and butter. Sear each side of the chops until rare.

Remove to a shallow baking pan and bake in a 350-degree preheated oven for about 12–14 minutes or until desired doneness. Allow to rest for 5 minutes before serving.

WILD RICE PILAF

Add everything to a large pot or rice cooker and follow the directions on the wild rice package, substituting chicken broth for water.

❧ YIELD ❧
Serves 2

RESTAURANT INDEX

RECIPE INDEX

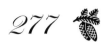